ADVANCE PRAISE FOR
INTRINSIC ~~EXCELLE~~NCE

"The subject of personal ~~training is more than~~ the physical. Having worked wi~~th~~ ~~...~~ for well over 30 years, in my opinion Rolando Garcia III has uncovered the keys to success. Not only as a personal trainer but for business success in general. Partnership, preparation, integrity, learning, strategy, and planning are only some of the keys to Rolando's success. I recommend this book for every aspiring trainer along with any individual who strives for success!!!!"

—**JOE ABRUZZESE**, President of ads and marketing, *Discovery Communications*

"Rolando Garcia is one of the most brilliant minds the personal training industry has ever known. Like myself, Garcia has risen to the top of the game in one of the most competitive markets in the world: New York City. That's no easy task.

The 4C Method is the voice of years of experience, expertise and common sense. A trainer's role is hard to define, but Mr. Garcia really 'gets it'. Rolando knows that what really makes or breaks a training career is not just the caliber of your workouts, but also your ability to master customer care, client acquisition and personal training sales. Rolando Garcia is clearly an expert on the science of training; what makes him unique is his expertise on business development and strategy. If you are entering the industry and do not know what to expect, you *have* to buy this book!"

—**DANNY KAVADLO**, author, *Everybody Needs Training*

INTRINSIC EXCELLENCE

BUSINESS DEVELOPMENT AND LEADERSHIP SYSTEMS FOR SUCCESS IN PERSONAL TRAINING

ROLANDO GARCIA III

DRAGON DOOR PUBLICATIONS

INTRINSIC EXCELLENCE

© Copyright 2016, Rolando Garcia III
A Dragon Door Publications, Inc. production
All rights under International and Pan-American Copyright conventions.
Published in the United States by: Dragon Door Publications, Inc.
5 East County Rd B, #3 | Little Canada, MN 55117
Tel: (651) 487-2180 | Fax: (651) 487-3954
Credit card orders: 1-800-899-5111 | Email: support@dragondoor.com
Website: www.dragondoor.com

ISBN: 978-1-942812-04-3
This edition first published in March, 2016
Printed in China

Book design by Derek Brigham | www.dbrigham.com | bigd@dbrigham.com

DISCLAIMER: The authors and publisher of this material are not responsible in any manner whatsoever for any injury that may occur through following the instructions contained in this material. The activities, physical and otherwise, described herein for informational purposes only, may be too strenuous or dangerous for some people and the reader(s) should consult a physician before engaging in them. The content of this book is for informational and educational purposes only and should not be considered medical advice, diagnosis, or treatment. Readers should not disregard, or delay in obtaining, medical advice for any medical condition they may have, and should seek the assistance of their health care professionals for any such conditions because of information contained within this publication.

THIS BOOK IS DEDICATED TO ALL PERSONAL TRAINERS—

BOTH EXISTING AND ASPIRING—

FOR ALL THE HARD WORK THAT YOU DO,

AND ALL THE INSPIRATION

THAT YOU GIVE TO YOUR CLIENTS.

CONTENTS

ACKNOWLEDGEMENTS

T he sum of a person's life can be defined by their decisions. Though much of them are the product of one's own doing, I personally believe that we are also greatly influenced by those who decided to invest their thoughts and feelings to our own growth, development, and overall success as individuals. Admittedly, there are those who may unwittingly influence our lives without intending to do so, even without the immediate knowledge of our own existence (like, in my case, I have been greatly influenced by Bruce Lee, Shakespeare, and Jim Collins—none of whom I have ever met).

That said, the individuals that have had the greatest influence over my life did not necessarily write a canon of plays like Shakespeare, write perhaps the greatest series of MBA books in recent history like Jim Collins, or completely revolutionize modern self-defense and invent a film genre like Bruce Lee. What these quiet individuals did, instead, was shape my life by including me in their own—their experiences, their insights, their feelings—by investing in who I am more-so than in what kind of success I would achieve. When I rose they cheered, when I stumbled a little they didn't make a big deal out of it. They molded me by believing in me. In their eyes, I was a champion before I entered the ring, a scholar before making the grade, a winner even though I had not won anything of worthy reckoning. Though I take the highest accountability in the life I have chosen to live, I know that without the great influence of these following individuals, I would not be blessed with the life I am living today.

My father taught me many things in my life. An attorney by trade, a fiction writer by aspiration, and a philosopher at heart, he taught me how to think. A loving and patient man, he taught me most importantly that the first consideration in any endeavor is cost. I, on the other hand, considered return as the first consideration. Together, he and I were able to dissect and analyze most things—poetry, business, martial arts, and philosophy. He always saw what it would cost, and I always saw what the rewards would be. With both perspectives at play, I learned to see the bigger picture. I am lucky to say that my father is my most important teacher.

My mother taught me the wisdom and strength of the heart. She taught me that it is the mind that seeks justice, that knows right from wrong, but it is the heart that brings understanding. A high-ranking officer in banking, I learned from her that single-minded determination will overcome most anything, even our deepest fears.

My parents are fierce individuals, but as a team they became indomitable. It is through them that I learned to love, live, and learn fiercely and unapologetically.

My brothers Jojo and Joel, the best brothers anyone can ask for. My older brother taught me "You can't love anyone unless you love everyone." My younger brother taught me "You can't be special unless you believe everyone is special."

Sifu Armando Basulto, created an environment that allowed for constant learning under extreme duress. In the five years of hard training I spent with him, it is only upon reflection do I realize that he kept instruction to a bare minimum. Instead he established the parameters of the scenario, defined the task, gave us the tools, then simply allowed us to be creative individuals, offering advice when needed, with individual growth trumping the often tempting ambition to promote a system or school. No pushing, no urging, no anxiety-ridden sales pitch about getting the next belt and buying the next uniform, he instead allowed us to relax, be calm, and think clearly while managing the internal and external pressures of an unrehearsed fighting scenario. These years laid the groundwork for the calm, analytical thinking I eventually developed and relied upon when pressure remained high and constant in the field of personal training.

There are many others who have influenced the ideas in this book, as well as my own success and development. Should you read this book and smile warmly, know that you have contributed mightily to what this is, and what I hope it can become.

Lastly, I thank my beautiful fiancée, Michelle Roth. Thank you for your love, your support, and your limitless faith in me.

FOREWORD

By Dan John

"**M**astery of your art cannot be confused with success in the profession. This adage is applicable not only in boxing, but in any professional field. And personal training is no exception."

There are times a poem or a quote simply stops you in your tracks. The first time I heard Dylan Thomas's "Do Not Go Gentle Into That Good Night," I realized that poetry can speak to the heart and send the imagination flying.

When I read this quote above from Rolando Garcia III's book, *Intrinsic Excellence*, I stared out my window on this perfect, snowy winter day in Utah and traveled across my life and personal history and realized that I had just read a new bit of truth:

"Mastery of your art cannot be confused with success in the profession."

Stories of actors, artists and musicians who have great talent and beautiful skill, yet are working 9 to 5 while waiting for their "break" have become cliché. Success demands ensuring—as the Trappist Monk Thomas Merton taught us—that once we climb to the top of the ladder of success, we find ourselves on the right wall.

Success is not the same as achieving a goal. Both the trainer and the client need to understand this early, but Garcia's book emphasizes this point throughout the text. Losing money, being in the red, is no way to be a personal trainer—and nor is ignoring the client or simply yelling negative comments. Most of us know this. The "How" of learning this is *Intrinsic Excellence*.

Garcia challenges the reader early...and often. My first wake up call came when we approached his Four Competencies: Technical Expertise, Business Development and Strategy, Customer Care, and Sales.

"What most personal trainers have missed by making these simple assumptions is that 75% of what actually drives professional success in personal training has nothing to do with personal training."

I'm a "25%er," and so are many of the people I know who love the gym, studio, center, spa and club. We love the community, the camaraderie, the smells, the language and the results. We may master the nuances of the squat and press, but Garcia blends a mixture of gut punches and fun narratives to guide the personal trainer from simply being a person who likes the gym to someone who is a successful businessperson. Skipping that 75% seems like a good way to go out of business.

And, most personal trainers barely last over one year. They skip the 75%.

Garcia completely rethinks the idea of goal setting. He keys in on an important truth: most coaches and trainers get excited about goals like "running a faster race," "benching more," or winning some championship. It ties into the performance side of the fitness world that came from the birth of lifting.

Something like "I want to weight X" or "I want to lose 15 pounds" may have a narrative behind the story. Maybe at that bodyweight, Edna fell in love, got married and all her dreams came true. That bodyweight reflects something much deeper and more personal than some performance level.

Although not bursting with acronyms, Garcia uses several excellent ones that would make great wall art. "PACT" should be instantly memorized by anyone coaching or teaching: Praise, Assist, Coach, Teach. He reviews looking at the positive things that the client is doing, including simply showing up. This section, Customer Care, ties in nicely with the section on Technical Expertise. Technical Expertise is the area most of us consider the foundation of training people, including assessment and program design.

But what good is a perfect program if the client doesn't know what to do and only receives negative feedback? Without Customer Care, the program is garbage.

One delight in the book is the cast of characters we meet in Garcia's travels. I think we all know Ryan and Hal, but many of us have met our share of Tanks and Lionesses, too. Their stories keep the book on pace and fun to read. Their stories are especially helpful in understanding the tool kits in Business Development and Strategy and Sales. Tank's sales stories might be the most enjoyable to read.

The last chapter may be Rolando's best. He discusses the transformative power of proper physical conditioning. One can't find a better line than:

"To be a part of helping someone believe in themselves that they become capable of living their lives with courage and dignity, is what makes what we do respectable, noble, and, in the final reckoning, worthwhile."

And this book is certainly respectable, noble and worthwhile.

—**Dan John**, author of *Never Let Go*

INTRODUCTION

How many times a year do you go to see your doctor? Once a year? Twice perhaps? How about your attorney (if you have one)? How about your financial planner? Your accountant? Your barber or hair-stylist? How often have you seen any of these professionals in the space of one year?

Think about this: personal training clients see their trainers roughly 2-3 times a week, which amounts to about 8-12 times a month. Based on these numbers, a personal training client will see their personal trainer somewhere between 96-144 times a *year*—that is more times than you see your doctor, lawyer, barber, accountant, and financial planner in one year *combined*. More significantly, you probably do not see your own relatives (outside of immediate family) that many times in one year.

You see your clients more often than any other professional— perhaps more than anyone else in their lives. This is the primary significance of the role that you play. Your role increases in significance when you consider that your clients come to you in order for you to help them achieve optimal health and fitness goals. As a trainer, you have the ability to help them lower body fat composition, improve cardiovascular health, build lean body mass, improve posture, and have an overall positive outlook in their life. You are capable of inspiring them to new heights, and encouraging them when setbacks and challenges give rise to self-doubt. You are not just an expert at what you do—you are also an inspirational model for the level of athleticism and poise that they aspire to achieve. You understand that authentic growth and development can only be had through sincere effort as opposed to theory, education through experience and dedication, and that it is important to embody all the virtues that you espouse by, first and foremost, being the greatest influence on yourself, thereby expanding that influence unto others. The impact that you have on the lives of your clients is infinite and immeasurable when you take into account these established and unassailable facts.

I hope that you are taking all of that to heart, because it is the plain truth. Give yourself the chance to think this over, and your own perspective on your growth and influence should change, for the better. More important, this is the time for you to consider what success means to you, then to go on and succeed on every imaginable level. At your very best, you have the ability to embody that elusive alchemy of athleticism, intellect, and singularity of purpose that, throughout human history, has been the cornerstone of success for every civilized culture and society. In many ways, you represent a resurgent ideal— that of a self-possessed individual who excels in physical abilities and intellectual capacity. However, you also chose your profession on the basis that it presents a greater challenge—a challenge to the spirit. It is not enough for you to be at your physical and intellectual peak, but you chose to also share your successes with your clients, in the hopes that they too can overcome their challenges with the same confidence and assuredness that you have. You believe in yourself, and you want others to believe in themselves, so that they can achieve a level of success that they had once thought impossible to achieve.

This is your mission, and the mission of everyone who chooses to become a personal trainer. And it is for this reason alone that you must succeed completely in your chosen field—for yourself and for your clients. Personal training is a challenging and completely demanding field. Few can handle its rigors; even fewer have the passion and ambition to succeed. Becoming successful has to be the only thing on your mind.

WHAT IS SUCCESS IN PERSONAL TRAINING?

You achieved your initial success in physical excellence by believing in yourself. You believed that you have the capacity to train, the discipline to endure, the passion to be motivated, and the ability to finish and achieve. You were not born as an athlete, let alone an expert. However, you developed yourself through focused and constant training. Through those rigors and challenges, you developed an invaluable belief in yourself that not only would you achieve your goal, but that it would be worth the sacrifice. This is the initial success of every personal trainer—through fitness and exercise you have exercised command and dominance over your life. It is a really great feeling, and one that is worth its weight in gold.

You may believe that you chose your profession because of your love for fitness and exercise. You love the gym environment and being surrounded by the dynamic energy. From my experience of interviewing viable candidates for personal training, I have found that the majority of you, especially those who succeed in this profession, enter the field with a passion for fitness, but what you really love is helping people achieve their own success. You love seeing the initial tentativeness and timidity of a client, seeing them overcome their challenges and fears progressively in time, and then ultimately come out victorious by achieving their goals. What you ultimately love is seeing everyone succeed. This is one of your defining features: success for you is neither complete nor satisfying unless it is shared with and achieved by others.

In other words, once you have reaped the benefits of believing in yourself, you want others to reap the same benefits. The very best in this field are those who believe in their clients' abilities to succeed, even when those same clients do not believe in their own capacity for success. This, along with your proficiency in changing your clients' physical appearance and athletic capabilities, defines your ultimate contribution as *success agents*.

THE FINANCIAL CONSIDERATION—
BUT ARE YOU *COMPLETELY* SUCCESSFUL?

Are you making the money you want as a personal trainer? Are you satisfied with your current income? Do you know how your business actually works, so that you know what is driving you into abject failure or holding your back from the success you dream of? It is important for you to be honest with yourself when you ask yourself these questions, because this book can help you better if you are.

Success and failure are not the only considerations when it comes to managing your personal training business. You must define what success is, and make it your complete focus. You must define what failure is, and be very mindful of its constant possibility. Most importantly, you must know HOW you will succeed, and how you will prevent failure. If you want to be a fitness professional, this must slowly but methodically become your way of being.

In order for this process to take place, you must achieve the first and most serious consideration in your field: FINANCIAL SUCCESS. Your business has to be profitable, because you completely believe in your business and its potential. This book is written for you, the fitness professional who possesses these beliefs and desires to become successful in your business. Financial success, much like success in fitness and exercise, is determined by the individual's starting point, environment, their unique challenges, and ability to recognize opportunity. Losing 15lb has a different meaning for someone who has lost it before vs. someone who has never lost a pound in their lives. For the former, success is a somewhat inevitable outcome, based on previously having achieved the feat. For the latter, every pound lost presents a type of Everest-like achievement.

It is the same for all personal trainers who are on this mission. For some, financial success is a simple, task-oriented process. For others, it can be emotionally-laden, stressful, and can prove to be more challenging than originally anticipated. Money (and its acquisition) has no real absolute value, but its acquisition is translatable to furthering your definition of success.

To put it simply, whatever perspective you may have about money, you need it in order to make your business successful. That is your goal. You also need it in order to achieve your true and more fulfilling definition of success, which is to be able to put your clients' needs first, without the slightest consideration for your own financial needs, which may hinder you with proceeding in earnest.

Along similar lines, regardless of your personal commitment and high level of proficiency in your chosen field, if your business as a personal trainer is not profitable and does not meet your financial needs, you will be forced to abandon it. You will have no choice but to call the endeavor a loss, and take on another job that may or may not be as fulfilling. This, in many ways, should not be acceptable to you, because you will never be able to justify to yourself why you had to leave personal training. You have invested too much time and financial resources into your education, then to only leave because somehow it didn't become profitable the way you envisioned. More importantly, with your clients achieving results, they too have invested substantially in your ability to deliver. Losing you would be devastating to most, if not all, of them. No matter how successful your partnership is with your client in terms of achieving their results, if you have not reached *your* results, your level of sustainable financial success as a personal trainer, you will be forced to abandon your business, your profession, your loyal clients, and the field that you love. In other words, no one wins in a scenario where your choice to become a personal trainer does not turn out to be a lucrative one. If you lose, everyone loses. If you fail, everyone fails. If you accept losing and failure as acceptable, you are not ready to be a professional. At the end of the day, you must succeed financially as a trainer, because your mission as a trainer depends on it.

Lastly, there is one final consideration to financial success that is worthy of careful thought and deep reflection. The partnership between you and your client can be healthier and more fruitful if you are financially successful, because your client's esteem of you depends on it. Your client will view you as someone organized, goal-oriented, efficient, resourceful, and intelligent not only because you are capable of helping them achieve their goals, but you are also capable of achieving your own. They respect the fact that you are capable of managing a business. Financial independence is a respectable benchmark of success, a noteworthy achievement, and something that, should you achieve it, you will share with your client, as they too have most likely achieved financial independence in their own field (or else they would not be able to afford your fees). Without this component of your success in place, your client will be less focused on their goals and achievements: they will end up worrying about how long you can keep going. They will be more worried about you quitting. They will start to worry about your financial stability, because they will begin to wonder how long you intend to train them before calling the whole thing off. Your client is now more concerned about you giving up, as opposed to whether they may give up. The partnership, at this point, will be less effective because both of you will be focusing on the feasibility and sustainability of the relationship, when the real focus of the relationship should only be about one thing: *the journey both of you have chosen to undertake to change both your lives.*

Your mission will only succeed if every possibility for its failure is mitigated by careful planning, judicious decision-making, and inhuman dedication. This applies to every aspect of your business, every aspect of who you are.

THE DISCIPLINE OF BUSINESS

Success, for yourself, starts with reconciling the passion-driven ideals with the expectations of a modern structure of a society. In other words, financial success should serve as the foundation for complete success in your profession. You cannot begin to call yourself successful as a personal trainer if you are not able to achieve your financial goals that will give you the luxury of freedom—to be creative in your field, and to do so with integrity. More importantly, your mission to help others will be more believable and enjoyable because you have already achieved a level of comfort and security that affords you to be compassionate and understanding. If you are not achieving your financial goals as a trainer, you will be distracted from your mission by mundane, modern-day constraints—bills, expenses, housing, and retirement planning. If you are not meeting your financial goals, buying lunch will feel like a max effort. Every training session will feel like a final lap around the track. Every day at the gym will feel like your last; every session will feel like a chore. You will wear your desperation on your sleeve. It is far more difficult for you to help others with their struggles when you yourself are struggling. There is no virtue in struggling for the sake of struggling. There is nothing to learn from failure, and everything to enjoy when success is achieved.

Should you focus solely on program design and efficient implementation of the training session (which is what we are paid to do) as the cornerstone of your success, you are losing sight of what is actually going to make your *overall* business profitable. These other drivers of business success require the same level of attention (and in some instances more-so). Many in the field are only passionate about a particular aspect of their business—the training session. It is a fine showcase for their skills, their knowledge, while the client is the immediate recipient of their existing repertoire. When trainers are training their clients, they are essentially doing what they love to do.

Quite frankly, loving your job has nothing to do with managing a successful business. Managing a successful business requires more than love—precision, focus, discipline, vision, planning, and persistence, to name a few. Anyone can love their job, anyone can claim to enjoy what they do, but few are tough enough to thrive in the discipline of business. Even fewer can claim to be successful.

As personal trainers with a passion for the ideal, many often find themselves on the compromising-end of doing what they love while "making ends meet." How often have you found yourself struggling? In personal training, there is the all-too-familiar struggle to find clients who will pay the appropriate fees. Once these clients are found, there is a daily struggle for clients to understand and appreciate hard-earned expertise, which can change their lives drastically for the better. To further complicate matters, the trainer's business has not met expectations, and there seems to be no solution in sight. To put it simply, it is hard to understand why such well-intentioned efforts seem to routinely fall, unfailingly, on deaf and unsympathetic ears, and how this failure can so deeply affect the growth and sustainability of their business's revenue. It seems so unfair, but it is a reality that many personal trainers face.

Here's a familiar scenario:

- A prospective client has called upon you for an initial consultation. They explain very clearly that they are currently unhappy with their weight and their appearance. They further explain that just 10 years before, they were in the best shape of their lives doing nothing but jazz exercise classes, some running, while partying all night and not caring for what they ate. They are in desperate need of regimented and purposeful training, because they also recently came from surgery after hurting their shoulder from an innocuous fall.

- They cite their goals to you—heart-achingly so. They would like to lose 20lb before their high school reunion which is 8 months from now, and they would just love to be who they were "before."

- Furthermore, the prospective client explains to you that they are on a budget, because they have kids, and their spouse is cutting back on expenses.

We clearly see that you have worked diligently to address the needs and requests of this particular client. In fact, you are supremely confident in your ability to train this individual and help them achieve their goals. To add to your confidence, your passion to help others drives you to give this prospective client your absolute best.

Here is the follow-up scenario:

- You tell the prospect that you will complete their assessment that day, to measure baseline fitness levels that will define (for both of you), where the client's strengths are, where their areas of development are clear, and what strategy you can both implement.

- Once the results are in, you tell the client that you need a day to go over the reports, in order for you to create a customized program that will address the needs of the client, as well as address their requests.

- Two days later, the client comes back, excited, eager, but a little nervous. You reassure them that the program will be fun, and they will benefit greatly from it.

- The session proceeds and you give clear instructions. The client acquiesces, and now they are moving, sweating, breathing, lifting, and moving some more. You check-in with the client in terms of how they feel, where they feel it, and if they see the benefit of these exercises. The client agrees wholeheartedly that this is perhaps the BEST training session they have ever had.

- After the session, you sit with the client and discuss the subsequent fees. You explain the purpose of the program, how it will benefit them, and how an investment in their health is smart, beneficial, and ultimately fulfilling.

Predictably, this is what happens next:

- The client explains that they cannot afford the fees, though they see the value of the exercises and appreciate your dedication.

- They recently explained to you that they are cutting back on costs as a household, so your fees are, quite frankly, an exorbitant luxury based on their current budgeting for the year.

- They then communicate if you could, perhaps, either a) give them a break on the pricing, or b) give them a sample circuit that they can implement on their own.

- You then counter by saying that they are worth it, that the benefits far outweigh the costs, and that the prospective client should cut back on other necessities without compromising their health.

- The client then counters by saying that they will discuss it with their spouse, and that they loved your "workout."

One of the important ambitions of this book is to clearly define not only what success is in personal training, but to also define the parameters wherein that success is achieved. Describing the "lay of the land" will help give you a set of realistic expectations, and allow you the opportunity to derive insights for yourself as you bravely hew your own path towards financial and complete success in your field. More importantly, you will then be able to translate that sense of passion and determination in all aspects of managing a business, so that success can be more greatly guaranteed, and mistakes mostly avoided. We learn from mistakes, and they are ultimately inevitable and valuable. We cannot, however, learn from failure. Failure is a series of mistakes. Although we can learn from our mistakes if we catch them early, failure is something we can only move forward from.

With a clear definition of success within the specific parameters of your chosen field, you can do your job courageously, creatively, and with total integrity.

COMPELLING AND INSPIRATIONAL LEADERSHIP

Achieving success for yourself is the result of competency, focused ambition, resourcefulness, adaptability, and efficiency. However, sharing that hard-earned success so that others may develop and benefit from it is the beginning of something altogether different. It is the beginning of leadership. Success builds a level of confidence that is felt simply by being in the presence of that individual. Before uttering a word, you can sense that in this unique person lies a distinct capability to see the best in themselves, thereby giving them the ability to see the best in others, finding solutions where others see problems, creating opportunity where others see dead-ends, elevating strengths where others may simply resort to managing weaknesses and offsetting liabilities.

Before a client entertains the idea of starting their journey toward their goals, you already see the capacity for discipline, the determination to succeed, and the strengths they can bring to the table in order for them to enact the change that they are seeking. Whether you know it or not, training a client goes beyond the simple skill set of outlining a set of exercises in a particular order, determining the sets and reps, and instructing your client through the day's session. A good majority of that session involves motivating and inspiring clients to do what often seems difficult and awkward, which then makes the client hesitant, if not outright unwilling to complete the exercises. To complicate matters further, the series of exercises may be completely easy for you. Instead of berating the client, you motivate them through positive reinforcement and instruction, and this is what separates you from most other professionals in the fitness field: you motivate and inspire the client through difficult tasks by communicating to them *at their level*. This is where you *connect* with them on a very human level by making the effort to understand their difficulties, showing an earnest effort to listen to what they are saying. To a certain extent, this is heartfelt compassion and genuine listening. This is a leadership skill. This is the same skill that managers utilize when they need their teams to produce, the same skill that the most inspiring leaders utilize to mobilize their constituents to action, regardless of the challenges ahead.

It is important for you to understand this at a very deep level, because what you are actually developing during a client's training session, aside from progressing them towards their goal, is a very significant life skill for *yourself*—the skill of leadership. This is the beauty of your profession, the true "win-win" of what we do—as you are developing your client, you are also sharpening yourself. This is why you cannot fail in this business: there is too much to lose if you do not succeed. By helping others, you are helping yourself become more compassionate, more inspiring, and more determined. If you fail, you will no longer have this opportunity for growth.

During modern times, the fitness arena and the gym were generally populated by professionals who focused on developing a specific physical aesthetic. Much of what is pervasive in gym culture today comes from that initial wave of gym enthusiasts who lifted weights and enjoyed aerobics, training for the purposes of achieving a particular look that conveyed fitness, athleticism, and raw magnetism. In fact, most gym members still subscribe to the same fitness standards and ideals that this initial wave of bodybuilding and aerobics enthusiasts brought to the fitness industry—still chasing after a pump and burn in the hopes of stilling an unsteady sense of self-worth. This is in stark contrast to the fitness professional of today. Today, the industry rests upon the confident shoulders of those fitness leaders who are in the field, day after day, helping to motivate and inspire their clients to achieve their absolute best, beyond what may appear on the surface, in order to face the challenges within. These fitness leaders are less concerned about achieving a physical aesthetic, but more so towards cultivating physical and intellectual excellence—complete success. For these individuals, strength is developed and sharpened but rarely used. There is a physical elegance that denotes assuredness, a palpable equilibrium that is felt by those in their proximity. Their physiques, as a result, convey a quiet restraint that is above showmanship and vulgarity. There is calmness and determination in their voice, in their movements, in how they manage even the simplest of matters. Self-accountability is their personal code; their goals and directives are self-assigned and self-determined. Most importantly, with the field being as competitive as it is now and far more in demand, these individuals take the opportunity to maximize their efforts in order to turn their practice into a legitimate and lucrative business. This is the fitness leader of the future; this is the personal trainer of our time.

As you read this book, you will realize that this personal trainer is you. This fitness leader is who you are aspiring to become. You are searching for a deeper sense of fulfillment that only complete success in personal training can bring. You must be determined enough to achieve this success that you are seeking, so that you read these pages with an open mind and a willingness to learn. Additionally, you are now more aware than ever that much more is riding on your success than your own sense of achievement and personal gratification. Your clients' achievements also rely upon your ability to succeed, financially and professionally. They have committed a substantial amount of their money, their time, and their trust upon your ability to train them, and the compassion that you bring to each session that they attend.

Most importantly, understand that the system in this book was designed and proven to help trainers like you succeed. As much as your own personal determination contributes greatly to your success, an effective method can help focus and streamline it so that your efforts are not wasted by trial and error. Combined with this method, your willfulness and ambition should lead you to financial success along with a deep sense of fulfillment that the work that you have chosen to do actually changes people's lives for the better. Be forewarned that this can only happen if you have the guts and the toughness to truly manage a successful business, through its highs and lows, through the victories and unexpected turns, which will test every ability you have, and your willingness to see this through. Understand the method, because it can only increase your belief in yourself. And every journey starts with you believing in yourself. Never forget this.

The 4C Method

Technical Expertise

Business Development & Strategy

Customer Care

Sales

QUALITY VS. COMPETENCY

The method in "Intrinsic Excellence" is called The Four Competencies method. It is a proven method of professional success in personal training. It produced high-performance trainers with high-income businesses. It turned two personal training divisions from historic lows into record-breaking highs. This definitive approach all but guarantees the dedicated fitness professional the ability to achieve high levels of success in personal training that is well within their reach, while creating opportunities for growth that go outside and beyond their current field. This approach should be exciting for every personal trainer because it clearly defines what is necessary for success, how to specifically achieve that success, but most importantly how that success directly affects your personal development and growth as well as those of every individual whose lives you happen to come across.

This is the system that will make you into a successful personal trainer by helping you understand what drives your personal training business.

The 4C Method first and foremost sets out to achieve definitively what competencies are necessary in order to become successful in personal training. It is not a list of descriptions; it is a template of necessary skills. Success for personal trainers tends to be illustrated by what an observer basically describes off-hand—the individual understands anatomy, creates good programs, is warm, friendly, and approachable. This individual is also dynamic, cheerful, and smiles at everyone. They also workout all the time. This individual never has a bad day and is always ready to help. This individual is prompt and punctual, open to feedback, knows how to cue his clients during exercises, and understands learning styles in order to adjust the intensity and exercise selection for the individual client. The individual must also have clearly defined goals for financial success in the field, and be ready to be patient to allow that success to....

These descriptions are, quite frankly, useless. They are some of the most useless pieces of kitchen sink hogwash that has ever tried to pass itself off as sound and effective business advice. The minute you hear this type of advice, nod your head and walk away, because whoever is disseminating this knows nothing about the business and what drives it towards success. These descriptions are an endless list of common qualities, descriptive traits, and best practices that are easily observable but offer little in terms of effective insight, vision, and planning. It is akin to describing the success of financial executives and law partners: they are all really smart, they went to good universities, have nice houses and work hard, and are tough negotiators. They also tend to wake up early in the morning, and work long hours. Should you emulate any of these qualities and behavior, you certainly have a realistic chance at becoming successful in finance or law. This is canned malarkey, to put it mildly.

The description of success is not the reality of success, and if you, the personal trainer, are to achieve real success, you must define what DRIVES it. It is important for you to clearly and definitively understand that all descriptions of success are not indicators of comprehending that success. Anyone who tells you to smile during a session in order to get more clients has NEVER run a successful personal training business. None of the aforementioned qualities of successful personal trainers ("They workout all the time", "Never has a bad day and is always ready to help") have proven to be effective in getting more clients, retaining more clients, and driving a personal training business into the stratosphere. Why? The answer is very simple and conclusive—because there are just as many personal trainers with similar qualities who are absolute failures in this field. There are just as many well-built smiling failures on a personal training floor as there are successful ones.

What are the necessary *skillsets* for a personal trainer to become successful in their chosen field? What level of education is required? What level of proficiency? Do they need a national certification? Are their physical requirements, such as squatting 300lbs or running a mile in under 6 minutes? Do personal trainers have to look attractive? Is a degree in the field necessary? These are common and understandable questions, for anyone looking to enter the field of personal training. Do you know, without a shadow of a doubt, what the pre-requisites are for personal training, and do they directly affect your overall success as a trainer? More specifically, do these prerequisites directly impact your ability to acquire new clients, retain them, and have them train at a frequency that is sustainable for your bottom line while delivering quantifiable results for your client base? Do these prerequisites create the level of connectivity that enhances the overall experience for both you and your client?

Certainly there are industry pre-requisites that can be listed off quickly:

- National Certification
- Good physical shape
- Must workout
- Knowledge of the industry
- Friendly and approachable
- Ability to connect with all types of people

This is a short list of general items that paints a positive picture of what a trainer must possess in order to succeed in their field. In fact, let us pose the question differently: why *wouldn't* a candidate, who is nationally certified, is in good physical shape because they workout regularly and intelligently, possesses knowledge of the industry, and is friendly and able to connect with people be wildly successful in personal training? The picture of this trainer is rather compelling—a professional who is friendly, competent, knowledgeable, and is in good shape has every reason to succeed. On paper, they "have the goods." Let us go even further by asking this question: if you knew someone who fit this exact description, wouldn't you at least entertain the idea that this person, should they choose to become a trainer, become successful?

The problem with this approach, both from the perspective of the candidate, their potential clients, and their potential industry is that this description is inadequate, misleading, and ultimately damaging. The candidate is risking their fiscal opportunities and livelihood on their ability to be friendly, approachable, and be in good physical shape. The client is risking their health and wellness on this individual's list of seemingly attractive qualities, not including roughly $15k a year on personal training fees. More compellingly, the fitness industry seems to be far more preoccupied with promising and delivering on results, and less so on the more essential question at hand: *how are we determining that the fitness professional is capable of delivering on these results?* How does the client know they are capable? How does the candidate know that their trainer is capable?

How do YOU know you are capable?

In fact, an entire industry's revenue-making capacity is built on the same list of qualities for personal trainers—a list that has been assumed to deliver sustainable year-over-year results. IF the trainer has a certification, stays in shape by working out consistently, and is approachable, THEN clients will purchase sessions, will train regularly, should achieve results, will feel the need to purchase more sessions, and get more results, in perpetuity.

The problem lies in three places. One, as has been previously mentioned, there are just as many friendly and approachable personal trainers who are in shape, yet fail in the field. Often, the friendliest and most approachable trainer in any given gym is often the one who is the least busy, and has time to socialize with gym members. There are also just as many well-educated personal trainers who fail in the field. Secondly, as also previously mentioned, qualities are not skill-sets. The quality we are describing and observing does not explain the underlying mechanism that drives success (or at least our hope of its eventual arrival). Lastly, and most importantly, there has been a failure to accurately identify the necessary skills sets (not qualities) that will directly help the trainer, and translate their efforts into success.

The solution that the 4C method offers is that by identifying and developing all 4 competencies, you have given yourself the opportunity to develop into a successful *fitness leader*. You are someone who is capable of viewing your overall skill-sets, and how they contribute to each interaction, and how that can lead into successful management of your personal training business. This is a far more demanding approach than simply becoming an expert in fitness, because you are now being called upon to develop ALL the necessary skillsets that will put your business into a solid state of productivity.

A description of success, no matter how well-intentioned or well-described, is not an explanation of success. The 4C Method is a system that classifies all of those explanations and drivers, in order for the trainer to bring success not just for his client and his industry, but most of all for themselves.

Do not let a description of success fool you into thinking that it is an *indicator* of success. Be more vigilant and critical than that. By being more vigilant and critical, it will become apparent to you that a set of qualities are fundamentally different from a set of *competencies*. What this system has achieved, and what this book is designed to share, is a template of necessary and pre-requisite competencies in order to become professionally successful in the field of personal training. It is proven, it is effective, and you must follow it.

THE FOUR COMPETENCIES

Before success is achieved, it must first be defined. After it is defined, you can then specifically observe what drives it. For those who are interested in success that is reliable and repeatable, it is not enough that they achieve it. They must also have absolute mastery of how it was achieved. In personal training, the Four Competencies are as follows:

- Technical Expertise
- Customer Care
- Sales
- Business Development and Strategy

Most personal trainers go into the field invested in only one core-competency—technical expertise. Financial resources are steadily and constantly invested towards the acquisition of national certifications, or a degree in anatomy or exercise physiology, daily training regimens, an extensive library of exercise science books, nutrition, massage, etc. Each one falls into only ONE core competency: Technical Expertise. This assumption turns the personal trainer into a fitness expert, but it does not address the daily obstacles and overriding challenge of the fitness *professional*: building a successful and sustainable business. A fitness expert does not necessarily have to deal with the daily tasks of facing a client, sharing their knowledge, tracking purchases, and ensuring that strategic objectives are achieved and that productivity is on track for the year. The fitness professional manages all of this on a daily, ongoing basis. How effectively they manage their day has more to do with dealing with packed scenarios that do not call upon or have little to do with technical expertise.

- A prospective client wants to train, but deems the personal training fees exorbitant (Sales competency).

- An existing client does not feel motivated to train on a particular day, although they have been achieving phenomenal results with your program (Customer Care competency).

- Although you have a full roster of clients, upon reviewing your bank account, somehow you do not see your financial revenue growing the way you anticipated. (Business Development and Strategy competency).

What most personal trainers aspire to become is to become a fitness expert, but if they are to stay in the profession they have to become fitness professionals who are experts in managing a business. This is the reality that has to be accepted, studied, implemented, and ultimately mastered.

The two common assumptions that make most personal trainers come to this conclusion make sense on the surface. Firstly, proficiency in your chosen field is paramount. This is true, frankly, of any field or profession, but this truth has limited application—it is limited to *entry* into the profession. You have to know the difference between a biceps femoris and a biceps brachii. You have to know the difference between a muscle-up and a chin-up. However, once an individual has entered a profession, other more relevant core competencies come into play, should that individual want to have a lasting career. For example, a professional boxer must not only be a boxing master—they must also have superb strength and stamina, be telegenic and well-spoken when being interviewed for upcoming fights (and more importantly post-fight play by plays), and have a clear understanding of personal finance so that their earnings are not squandered later in life.

Mastery of your art cannot be confused with success in the profession. This adage is applicable not only in boxing, but in any professional field. And personal training is no exception.

Secondly, personal trainers tend to be focused on the core competency that they love and also gets them paid—the actual personal training session. Whether the personal trainer is freelance or works for a company, the trainer's hourly fee tends to be determined by a subjective (and somewhat arbitrary) criteria that takes into primary consideration the level of education that the trainer has achieved in *technical expertise.* Detrimental to this process is the fact that it takes into lesser consideration competencies in sales, customer service, and business development. Degrees in the field, along with prestigious national certifications, are taken into serious consideration when an hourly fee is determined for the services of the personal trainer. This process all but enforces that the trainer become an expert, as opposed to mastering the business. Though this perspective addresses the definitive bottom line, its narrow scope completely misses two primary objectives of long term success in the field:

- Acquiring and Retaining personal training clients that translates into financial independence (Sales, Customer Service, and Business Planning Oriented Scenario).

- Long-term opportunity for growth of the business, as well as the personal development of the fitness professional as they expand their scope of practice and sphere of influence (Leadership and Business Development Scenario).

What most personal trainers have missed by making these simple assumptions is that *75% of what actually drives professional success in personal training has nothing to do with personal training.* They are not aware that the profession requires hundreds of hours in customer care, sales, and business development scenarios where their advanced degrees and national certifications have limited capacity to be effective and simply do not apply.

Additionally (and perhaps more succinctly) what most fitness companies and organizations, and what an *entire* industry has completely missed is identifying and codifying the core competencies necessary in order to not only fulfill the job description of a personal trainer, but how a deep mastery of these core competencies can lead to overall financial success. By acknowledging that these Four Competencies are the major components that drive a personal trainer's success, what we have essentially done as an industry is transform our once passion-driven endeavor into a precise and disciplined business that has long-term viability for success for many decades to come. Personal training is a growing sub-set of a burgeoning industry, it is here to stay, and it is important for those who want to grow within the industry to understand that this is a tough and serious business.

THE TAKEAWAYS OF THE FOUR CORE COMPETENCY METHOD

- 75% of what drives a personal trainer's success has *nothing* to do with personal training.

- 75% of a personal trainer's continuing education curriculum should include subject mastery in sales, customer care, and business development/strategy

- Product innovation (mastery of technical expertise) is not the definitive solution for the majority of problems that the personal trainer encounters on their journey to success.

- The product that we offer is not the program we implement, but the fully-developed individual who delivers it.

75% of what drives your personal training business is your level of mastery of customer care, sales, and business development/strategy. This helpful and perceptive insight allows you to, firstly, understand the foundational components of what actually drives a personal training business. It is not as simple as teaching someone to lift weights and follow a nutrition program. Knowing what drives the business will help you to create solutions. It will also help you categorize problem areas that you encounter within their appropriate competency that pertains to it, thereby addressing it with the appropriate mindset. The first mistake that most personal trainers make (even the most seasoned veterans) is to approach every problem scenario from the perspective of technical expertise. If a trainer has a client retention issue (when a trainer loses a client), it is often addressed by learning a new workout, or getting another certification, or re-designing a program, when in fact it could be an issue attributable to:

- Customer Care (e.g. does the personal trainer possess authentic active listening skills, or, does the trainer leverage the strengths of the client with praise and positive reinforcement?).

- Sales (e.g. does the trainer understand the meaning behind an objection? Do they have the specific tools to address a specific kind of objection?).

- Business Development and Strategy (e.g. does the trainer understand what kind of impact the client's participation has on their revenue and productivity in relation to their relevant averages).

Having a thorough understanding of the Four Competencies Method gives you full and broad powers over your entire personal training business, beyond the hour that you are paid by your client. It allows you not only the ability to problem solve in an organized and logical manner, but to also proceed with your continuing education and development in a similar fashion. Your library must be equipped with books on sales, customer care, planning, development, negotiation, strategy, and management, along with your books on expertise, if you want to be completely successful in this field. You must make yourself diligent in tracking your overall *effectiveness*, rather than being focused on optimizing a specific but narrow *ability*. By having a library of books and resources that covers the scope of your professional competencies, you are positioning yourself for greater success that allows you to proceed with clarity and confidence.

With this in mind, it is evident that proceeding in continual study of technical expertise in your field, to the exclusion of study in customer care, strategy, and sales, will lead to quickly observable diminishing returns. Constantly investing in a competency that does not address what your business needs are can only be regarded as myopic and foolhardy. The discipline of business requires that you constantly manage the success of your business, persistently and with a sharp-eye for detail. You must do whatever it takes to guarantee the success of your business, which means knowing which competency to develop and leverage at the right time.

Part of this insistence on constantly adding to the technical expertise competency is your innate passion for fitness and exercise. There is a lingering hope that further expertise will have another relevant effect—the product we offer will be new and more exciting the more we study and develop this particular quadrant of our skill sets. If you study new exercise modalities and offer them to your clients, they may just help you in retaining them. They may even help in converting a few new clients. This mindset of innovating what may very well be a sound and effective product in the hopes of growing a stalled business is far from new. It is easily observable in the products you buy from your favorite companies. Every year, a new product comes out, with much fan-fare and anticipation, only to discover that most do not deliver on the innovations. What tends to be more disappointing is that the previous year's products may sometimes perform better than the new one.

Innovating a solid product is necessary to anticipate the needs of an existing market, and perhaps entertain the opportunity of creating new ones. However, this particular strategy is difficult to apply in your field, because your field is related to the sciences, which means that our success is greatly reliant upon proven and established methods. At the end of the day, there are only so many ways to lift a barbell in order to achieve commonly requested fitness goals. This, in essence, makes your approach to product innovation problematic – your product inherently *resists* innovation. The quality of your product is determined by the scientific proof that validates it. What you are actually delivering as a product is a *commodity*—a product that can be utilized across the industry, by any trainer, and has been proven effective to such a degree that the trainer (or company) that delivers it cannot differentiate itself merely on the product alone. In other words, if you want to set yourself apart in order to manage your business more effectively, you are better off innovating your *customer service, sales, and business development competencies* because that is the 75% that drives your business.

Here is a clear example of why your product is a commodity: every gym has a bench press. Every Monday is "International Bench Press Day". That means that every gym, regardless of brand affiliation or school of thought, will have this unofficial day where the majority of members will execute this exercise. You can go to as many certifications as you want that will help you optimize this particular exercise. You can even be a world champion at bench pressing. This achievement, however, will only differentiate you among bench press competitors, which will only narrow your market when you should be *expanding* it. More importantly, you will have neglected your studies in customer service, sales, and business development, which has been proven to be more effective in delivering solid results in growing and sustaining a personal trainer's business.

The mindset of the trainer who wants to more directly and effectively impact their business from the perspective of growth, must be able to manage their training programs as *commodities*, and focus their energies instead on *innovating their customer care, sales, and strategic approach*. This alone can revitalize your business and give you a greater sense of control over its growth and productivity. Utilizing a relatively new and effective sales strategy can invigorate even the most hardened of personal training veterans. Secondly, there is more opportunity for exponential growth in the business by innovating the 3 other competencies. Lastly, the library of books on these subjects is endless, innovative, and continually evolving. In other words, these subjects are dependent upon constant innovation, because business management requires innovative approaches in order to remain competitive and relevant. Do not differentiate your product—differentiate yourself!

HISTORY

In 2010, the personal training division I had been assigned to manage was on a two-year downturn. Though it had achieved record performances in 2008 in several key metrics (particularly in overall sales and productivity), the division's performance had gone south since its heyday. There were also several *associated* metrics that had been trending in a downward manner, which created conversations around the prevention of potential failure.

Failure is like a light mist that slowly and somewhat harmlessly settles upon the landscape. The initial acknowledgement is simply not there, so (early on) failure feels like a gentle and warm haze—there is little sense of impending harm that only a cold and firm grasp of reality can bring. That reality comes soon enough when we want to get out of failure and somehow cannot. We are lost in its maze. When we look up to the sky, we realize that we have not seen the sun for quite some time. When I was assigned to this PT division, there were glimmers of hope here and there, but there were several key concerns.

Firstly, clients were not training at a high enough frequency to bring about success for themselves, let along the trainers they were training with. Secondly, and more alarmingly, a majority of the division's trainers were not making enough money to make a decent living out of personal training. It seemed at the time, to me, that a lot of people were lost in this maze. The mist had not cleared, but with some investigation, there was a greater sense of the general landscape. At such moments, when a sense of clarity first arrives, it was important for me to resist the temptation to act upon initial data, in the hopes that urgency alone could help solve a pervasive and complex problem. This is because a problem cannot be solved when one is looking for a solution.

One must first become intimate with the problem, understand its mechanisms, its nuances, its history and unique temperament. After this, do not tolerate the problem—one must impose this mindset once a problem is clearly comprehended on every level. Then, you can start to simplify it, and the solution presents itself not just to you, but to anyone who glances at it. The elegance of a proposed solution is ultimately determined by its ability to simplify the problem it has been tasked to solve.

Once the early data came regarding percentages of staff and active clients, the urge to act came from all directions. Clients wanted different trainers because they were not happy with their results. Trainers wanted very much to succeed, but were at this point becoming frustrated with their own lack of results. To further complicate their situation, these same frustrated trainers insisted that some sort of intervention by management could alleviate their problems. Meanwhile, upper management took turns trying to solve the problems as well – trainers needed to be more dedicated and spend more time in the gym to get clients by prospecting on the floor. Along the same lines, we were advised to run contests and activities to get clients "more engaged", in order to drive productivity.

When people are lost in this mist of failure, they are at their most frantic when they get their first sense of the landscape. In this urgent and frenzied state, people search desperately for solutions, when they should in fact be looking for a deeper comprehension of the problem at hand. They do not have the patience to understand, reject, and ultimately simplify it. Urgency, in this sense, is the enemy of critical-thinking. The division had reached a turning point—everyone from clients to trainers to upper management knew that the division could do better, knew that the landscape was unsettling, that no immediate solution was available even though there was an urgent and overwhelming need for one. Like an army of displaced and desperate samurai, they wanted to kill *something*—if only they could find it. Swords were drawn, voices raised the alarum, but they only slashed the air. More often they slashed at each other.

In such situations, in the middle of this melee, it is important to keep one's sword sheathed. In such situations, it is important to walk calmly, to think clearly, to remove oneself from the chatter and meaningless noise, in order to patiently observe. Problems have a way of revealing their mechanisms, their hidden gears and levers, if one has the courage to face it for what it is. In this calmness, you will see a piece of this problem that will clarify your purpose and embolden you. Your insight into the problem is the beginning of creating your solution for it.

At the time, The Four Competencies Method was that valuable insight. It silenced many swords to return to their sheathes. The 4C Method became our way out.

INSIGHT BECOMES ACTION

When one observes a gym floor, especially when it is busy with trainers and clients, one makes a clear and obvious observation—it is hard to tell one from the other. We cannot tell who has invested 200 hours into their education versus someone with 2,000 hours into their education. We cannot tell who has a degree from one certification versus another certification. The matter becomes more complicated when they are doing similar exercises for their clients. There may be observable differences in how one trainer cues their client for a squat versus another, but that can also be a result of how that particular client responds to a particular style of cueing.

As a manager, one who has been tasked to drive the success of the division's clients and trainers, as well as achieve productivity and profitability goals, this observation became the starting point for the creation of The Four Competencies Method. By and large, trainers may vary greatly on paper with regards to their education and competency in their technical expertise, but on the field this is not so easily discerned. If a trainer's task is to cue a client to do a proper lunge, it matters little if that trainer has a degree in exercise physiology or if a colleague taught them how to cue a client for a lunge *if the net result is the same*—i.e. the client was able to complete the lunge *successfully*.

Similarly, one cannot tell if a person went to a prestigious university or dropped out of college when comparing billionaires if one is comparing *net worth*. There are billionaires without advanced degrees and billionaires with advanced degrees. It does not mean that an advanced degree is necessary in order to amass wealth. It also does not mean that dropping out of college will lead to billionaire status, although there are those who have accomplished this feat. All it means is that the observation of an *indicator* of success does not lead to a comprehension of what *directly contributed* to that success.

When it was observed that investment in acquiring greater technical expertise in personal training had diminishing returns when the trainer was on the field, it simply meant that other drivers for success were at hand, and had yet to be defined, codified, and ultimately taught. The main reason to search for these other drivers, these other core competencies, was due to the fact that the *productivity* and subsequent *fiscal* success varied greatly from trainer to trainer. There were many failing trainers who had the requisite certifications and advanced degrees. There were many successful trainers who had no college education, had common certifications, and had little interest in furthering their education.

Perhaps ideally one can say that a successful trainer is someone who can do both, and there are those who can. However, an achievable ideal does not invalidate a common and similarly achievable reality, especially if an intimate understanding of that reality helps understand the deeper mechanisms of overall success. With 86% of the failing division consisting largely of trainers who had few clients and little feasible income, it was important to understand how to drive *realistic* success before striving for and upholding an immaculate ideal. Everyone knows the ideal, but few can actualize success.

By observing varying degrees of performance and profitability from trainer to trainer regardless of their level of education in technical expertise, it became highly apparent that other core-competencies were at play. Customer Care was necessary for the trainer to ensure that each client was treated as an individual, especially if they voiced concerns that were not included in the textbooks. Customer care gives validity and integrity to the client's concerns. Sales training was also necessary in order for the trainer to manage objections, such as concerns regarding pricing, level of commitment, among other things.

Most importantly, trainers need to understand that Business Development and Leadership Systems need to be in place in order for them to fulfill the requirement of making the endeavor fiscally feasible for the long-term, as well as fulfill their role as leaders who are guiding their clients to their own success. Trainers with a sense of business development understand the cyclical environment within which their objectives must be achieved, with allowances for variances and opportunities to cushion in anticipation of foreseeable drops. At the heart of it all is the commitment towards leadership as the ultimate role that the trainer plays in the lives of everyone they come into contact with. Before they are fitness enthusiasts and professionals, they are committed to being leaders in the field.

As the division's manager, this insight led me to several innovative conclusions:

- Develop a thorough curriculum in furthering the education of trainers in these neglected core-competencies of Customer Care, Sales, and Business Development/Leadership.

- The curriculum needed to address each trainer's individual strengths and weaknesses, as it related to their core-competencies, and ensure that their development in each skill-set contributed to improved overall productivity and profitability.

- The methodology and subsequent curriculum must help define interviewing and hiring criteria, so that the division's overall success relied upon a growing group of trainers who understood the interplay of each core-competency.

The results were immediate and dramatic—the first batch of "4 Competencies" trainers were hired after my first month as head of division. Four months later, the division hit its sales and sessions goals. Two of the trainers in that first batch cracked the Top 5 spots in 3 months, achieving full-time status 2 months ahead of schedule.

The next few months became unprecedented – the division went on to achieve the longest winning streak in the location's history. More importantly, all-time productivity and profitability records were set. As more new hires went through the newly established method, more top producers kept coming out to establish themselves as successful professionals in their chosen field, to the ultimate benefit of the division. 2011 became a banner year for the division, but 2012 (my last year there before getting a promotion) proved the method's effectiveness even further:

- All-time record in sales
- 2nd highest record in productivity

From my batch of top producers, six were selected for promotion to managerial positions. Each top producer went on to become successful managers on their own, running their own successful divisions. The greatest achievement for the division, however, came in lifting the mist that had once confused a team that needed inspiration to facilitate effective solutions. In order to find these solutions, one must be courageous in seeing the problem for what it is, with a lens that brings clarity to a somewhat impossible task. That lens you are searching for is The Four Competencies Method, and it will bring you to the success you know you are capable of achieving.

THE FIRST COMPETENCY

TECHNICAL EXPERTISE

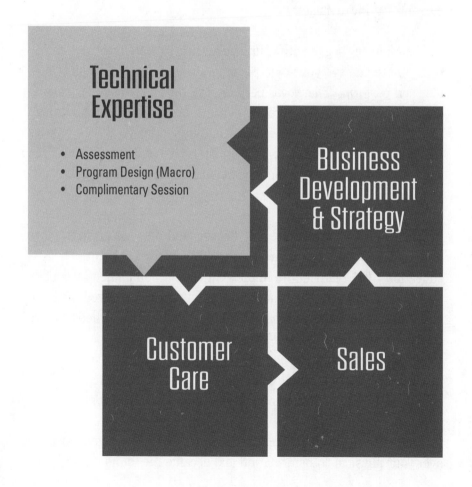

Technical Expertise

- Assessment
- Program Design (Macro)
- Complimentary Session

Business Development & Strategy

Customer Care

Sales

I n this chapter, you will explore the three components of the core-competency of Technical Expertise—Assessment, Program Design, and the Training Session, and how each component carefully works in tandem with the other, in order for the client to receive a greater sense of confidence in your ability to manage their fitness goals and aspirations.

The core competency of technical expertise is where you invest the majority of your resources as a professional: your numerous national certifications, your workshops and journals, your library of books on nutrition and biomechanics, and the new training modality that you are currently trying to master.

Your journey began with your love for fitness. You may have started by trying to achieve your own personal ideal of how you should look, feel, and perform. There was perhaps, at first, an element of trial and error. Some exercises were easy, some proved difficult. Through this process you found eventually what worked for you. The process that you underwent on the surface may have seemed a physical one at first, and perhaps later there came an emotional and psychological transformation as well.

Your journey, however, was deeper and in many ways more profound—you underwent a process of improvement through self-education. The many hours in the gym were accompanied by equally numerous hours of finding sources that could help you in your mission of getting more fit. At first, gym buddies and the local health store may have provided tips on exercises and nutritional supplements. Eventually magazines and popular books on the subject became trusted resources. In time you found more professional sources—college courses, national certifications, and specialized workshops.

As time went by, your continuing education became your priority over your physical transformation and became the foundation of your continued evolution towards a personalized ideal. Your passion for fitness is built on your endless fascination for the human body and its development, and how that development impacts every aspect of your life. Your passion, your discipline, your love for your craft intertwines with your personality, your life choices, and your identity. The depth of your commitment to your craft can only be equaled by your desire to see others reap the benefits of your experience and your knowledge. This is how your passion became your profession.

The very best personal trainers have the special ability to take their knowledge into their daily professional lives in a way that very few other professionals can do. They have a way of making their knowledge, a dynamic mixture of complicated science and hard-earned experience on the field, and the result of an on-going commitment to achieving health and fitness, accessible and even alluring to those who may initially have been intimidated by physical exercise. There is care in how the knowledge is disseminated, discernment in how it is further refined, and discipline in how one applies it.

When a client decides to invest their resources in training with you, the essential quality of your offering depends on how seriously you take fitness and exercise not only as a lifestyle choice, but as the unifying philosophy of your professional existence.

The technical expertise component of your overall set of competencies is not just the foundation of your chosen profession—it is the central philosophy of your approach to how you live your own life.

The technical expertise core competency is where you invest the majority of your resources as a professional. Think of anything fitness-oriented, and it falls conveniently in this category. Your numerous national certifications, your workshops and journals, your library of books on nutrition and biomechanics, and the new training modality that you are currently trying to master...each one falls into this particularly category.

For many, this is where the journey begins and ends. It is certainly the beginning, but far from an end. There is more, much more. In this chapter, you will explore the three components of this core-competency, how each component carefully works in tandem with the other, in order for the client to receive a greater sense of confidence in your ability to manage their fitness goals and aspirations.

THE LIONESS

The gym floor in an upscale New York City location is a thrill to behold. There is a driving music in the air that is both rhythmic and urgent. It can be heard even in the locker rooms, in the showers. Its inescapable pulsation becomes the soundtrack of a member's workout. Members move from one exercise to the next with enviable focus, to a constant beat. Treadmills are often at capacity, with members running or walking at varying speeds at different inclines, but all towards some distant but targeted destination that only their sweat and strict regimens will take them. There is a fierceness in the air that is both alluring and intimidating, and one cannot help but succumb to it. At this level, members are not only some of the most beautiful people one has ever seen, they are also some of the most successful people on the planet. CEOs as well as celebrities all come to a place where the only acceptable currency is focused effort, unquestionable self-confidence, and a subtle personal style.

It is here, where physical and mental endurance mix with the force of personality, that Susan decided to give herself the opportunity to succeed. It is here where she first set foot to become a personal trainer. Young and self-possessed, she found herself in the center of an unspoken race towards a tantalizing ideal of perfection. The first time she walked on the floor in her uniform, there was an unmistakable elegance to her gait. Whether she knew it or not, she was completely captivating and breathtakingly beautiful. Members took notice of her immediately. All eyes were on her, once she was on the floor. Tall with long dark blonde hair, she stood like a champion athlete of some impossible sport that was not made for the futile efforts of worshipful mortals. When Susan would pick up the heavy plates that members had left on the floor, she picked them up effortlessly, like they were rice cakes. Slim, strong yet very feminine, she had the qualities that would assure her the success that she desired.

Yet, inwardly, Susan doubted herself. She spoke in a gentle hush. Combined with her unmistakable physical presence, the paradox made her even more attractive, but her hush hid a story. Susan was an immigrant from Eastern Europe who but a mere five years ago could not speak a word of English. Her English was still not perfect. She also had an accent. Although she had a degree in nutrition and a master's degree in marketing, this thoroughbred worried that her English would stumble when she would try to talk to members, to connect with them so that they would hire her as their trainer. Her expertise alone would not convert these discerning and critical members to buy packages of sessions—packages that she desperately needed them to purchase, because she was determined to succeed.

She had to make this go at personal training successful and lucrative because her determination had a singular purpose: she had a sister back home who needed support as a single mother. Her sister had a three-year old son. Susan wanted to provide every opportunity for both of them, and in this new country she saw that she had that exact opportunity. When Susan would walk on the gym floor, she did not let this new world shake her self-confidence. Her family was depending on her confidence.

Eventually, as time went on, Susan got to know me better as her manager. I gave her a few tips here and there, but she knew I had a system. She eventually accepted me as her mentor. She wanted success, and she wanted the system that came with it. As time went on, she learned how to take her expertise and use it to connect with members. She had challenges along the way—she had to work, because the system made her work. More importantly, I demanded that she exceed herself—daily. There were many times she came to my office incredulous at the things I demanded of her. There were a few times she walked out in a huff. I kept at her. To everyone else, she was the captivating European beauty from another world. To herself, she was the determined single mother who could not help but sometimes doubt her ability to succeed.

But to me, she was none of that. To me, she was something else. When she finally surrendered to the tough journey I laid out for her, she achieved success that she had not previously conceived of or imagined. In her, I saw someone who could succeed with proper mentoring. In her, I saw something more primordial, more elemental.

To me, she was a lioness.

THE ASSESSMENT

The client assessment is your first opportunity to apply your knowledge as a personal trainer. From the assessment, you can gauge their willingness to invest, establish your expertise, ask important questions, and reach a fundamental agreement that will make your partnership beneficial for both of you. It is during the assessment that you learn about your client, and gather the relevant data that significantly affects the quality of the subsequent sessions, because that data feeds the decisions you make about your client's program, while you make them feel that you are similarly invested in them and their success.

During the assessment you are establishing a leadership role. Although this process does not have the same thrill compared to training the client on the floor, it is important nonetheless. If we consider, for a moment, that the primary mechanism that drives success in personal training is the quality of the relationship between trainer and client, which is determined by the level of commitment and communication between both parties, then the assessment process and how it is handled is, in fact, *the most important component of your entire technical expertise skillset*, because this is where that entire process starts.

The assessment is more important than the training session and the macrocycle and subsequent meso/microcycles that promise to deliver results for the potential client. For many years, the prevailing belief in the industry has been that the quality of the workout session is the most important component of the trainer's toolbox. This belief is pervasive on many levels, and it is predicated on one simple and observable fact—the trainer gets paid on a *per session basis*. If we are to look at the success of personal training solely from the financial end, then it is logical to conclude that the higher the quality of the session, the more financially beneficial it would be for the trainer. This process follows this line of thinking: if a trainer can continually improve the content, organization, and execution of a *training session* (by applying the lessons of continuing education workshops or adding new exercises and modalities), the quality of that session should continue to be raised.

This line of thinking, however, is predicated on the narrow-focus of improving the work we are paid for, as opposed to strengthening the *relationship* of the trainer and client. In other words, if your continued improvement as a professional is dictated solely by your desire to increase the quality of the training session, you are missing perhaps, the biggest opportunity to strengthen the overall relationship—the fitness assessment.

There may very well come a time when relevant metrics, such as body composition, resting heart rate, blood pressure, body weight, and the results of the pushup test, among others, can be simply inputted into a device that calculates them all into a sophisticated algorithm that produces an effective workout program that, should the client commit to it diligently, reap the intended results. There may very well come a time when exercise science and technology meet for the convenience of a client who simply wants to get in decent, reasonable shape. Data is fed, a prescription is made, the client follows the curriculum, and the intended results are achieved—conveniently and efficiently. Personal idiosyncrasies, inconvenient gym locations, expensive membership fees will be eliminated. Technology will never show up late for a training session or have a bad day, because its purpose is to deliver results efficiently and conveniently.

It's interesting to see how this transition to technology affected two other industries—clothing and watches. There was a time when clothing and watches were both handcrafted by skilled artisans. For both men and women these items were handmade. An entire wardrobe and its quality depended upon the craftsmanship of a tailor. Similarly, a wristwatch's accuracy and reliability depended upon the watchmaker's craftsmanship. For hundreds of years, quality craftsmanship determined the quality of the product that consumers of these two industries sought.

Later in the 20th century, several technological advancements in manufacturing allowed companies to make products on a mass scale that were more affordable, and with reduced costs on a per unit basis.

Convenience and efficiency were considered more desirable than traditional products that delivered similar results at a higher cost to the consumer. Now you would think that bespoke tailoring and hand-made Swiss watches would be relegated to the past. Neither should even be part of our lexicon, let alone serve any sort of cultural relevance in our society. Yet, as of this writing, there has been a massive resurgence in recent years for bespoke tailoring, limited production women's clothing, and hand-made Swiss watches. Clearly, people are willing to pay a premium for quality, uniqueness, and craftsmanship, on every level. Once relegated to mass extinction, both came roaring back from the past with more cultural relevance than ever before.

What does this have to do with your expertise as a trainer and your relationship with your clients? Drawing conclusions from these observations from two different industries is outside of the scope of this book. However, it is important to be mindful of how convenient access to the product and efficiency in producing its results is not that far from our industry either, considering the recent, awe-inspiring advancements in technology as it relates to fitness. More alarmingly, there may come a time when technology, similar to what happened in clothing and watches, may become better at collecting relevant baseline fitness metrics, designing a fitness program at a price well below our typical hourly rates, and deliver similarly effective results.

Should technology outpace us in delivering results, what value can we truly offer to our future clients when they can easily access similar workouts for a conveniently lower price?

The answer lies in what technology cannot offer and has never been able to offer in any industry: technology can never understand what it is to be human. Although it has the ability to make our lives more convenient, it lacks the ability to transform the individual on a more fundamental and emotional level, because it lacks the capacity to understand motivation, behavior, and human struggle. Only another person, one who has been through a similar journey of transformation, can do that. When your client has difficulty with a set of exercises, or their motivation is simply not there, all the advancements in technology cannot replace a few kind words of encouragement from a professional who has mastered the task, and understands the nature of their client's struggle. Though our potential clients work hard to earn their results, and continually search for better ways to optimize their ability to achieve them, their innate sensibilities ultimately guide their search towards the warmth of an understanding and knowledgeable soul. Our journey in fitness is, in actuality, an adventure in our essential struggle to master and come to terms with our own humanity. This is one of the primary reasons why the initial assessment is, perhaps, the most important component of the technical expertise skillset—it sets the tone for guidance and leadership that is based on understanding the human desire to achieve our unexplored potential.

Trainers who skip the initial assessment with their clients altogether lose this important opportunity for leadership and human connection. From there, the client has no sense of progress, direction, guidance, and overall reassurance—because there is no leader in place. It is understandable why so much emphasis is placed on the training session, but it comes at the cost of having a greater understanding of what motivates your client. For the true personal trainer and fitness leader, establishing the tone of the relationship early on will determine the nature of that relationship going forward. This perspective requires a far more long-term view, taking into consideration the potential ups-and-downs that both you and your client will experience, and how both of you will have to pull through it together. These ups and downs cannot be handled professionally without a comprehensive assessment in place, because the process of understanding what the client wants and needs was not there to begin with.

In this light, the assessment has to take a greater priority over the actual training session, because it establishes the mindset of leadership that is required for all personal trainers to uphold. You are constantly assessing your client because you are constantly making efforts to understand them, collecting soft data such as mood, breathing patterns, levels of perceived stress, along with hard data that gives you direct feedback on their ability to complete a series of tasks that you have given them, and how successfully the client is adapting to the program they are currently on.

Let us be clear—we are constantly assessing our clients within the framework of our expertise, in order to better lead them toward their goals and ultimate success.

A client can easily access a hard and challenging workout through various media and become better at that workout, but it takes a leader to help the client understand themselves within the context of their own difficulties. The transformation they seek occurs only when their understanding of themselves deepens. Technology can make them better, but understanding is what makes them transform.

MENTORING THE LIONESS

Susan had been sitting at the assessment room 30 minutes before our appointment. A natural perfectionist, she knew that she had to be ready for my review of her assessment. I had made her practice several times, so that she could effortlessly manage the technical aspects of the process. Body fat calipers can become cumbersome, forms can be disorganized, heart rate monitors can be misplaced—it was important for her to effortlessly manage the technical minutiae of her assessment, so that she could focus on the most important element of the process: the potential client in front of her and their list of needs.

When I arrived for our meeting, she smiled and shook my hand firmly. She was beaming with self-assuredness, and I could tell she was ready to begin. Before we started I asked her how she felt, and she said she felt absolutely fine. She thanked me for giving her so much of my time, for investing so much in her development, and that she was determined to not let me down. I assured her that I knew she would not, that she was a hard-worker, and that my faith in her was solid.

We then proceeded with the mock assessment. She asked me questions about my injury history, my favorite activities, my current fitness goals, and what exercises were my favorite. As I answered them, she jotted them down in her notes, making sure that my answers had been duly recorded. She was meticulous when it came to reviewing her notes, and this mock assessment was no exception. Susan could be timid at times, because of her limited mastery of English, but her nature was to be assertive and self-possessed, and these aspects of her personality showed themselves clearly and distinctly when she was taking note of my answers. She made me feel like nothing I said would escape her. She was a huntress.

At the end of our practice, I asked her how she felt about her practice, and how she did. She was, not surprisingly, very critical of herself. She felt her execution of the body fat calipers lacked precision, and that she fumbled a bit with the order of forms, which cost her time. She also felt that she lacked efficiency in executing the movement assessment, that it could have flowed more smoothly, more seamlessly.

I nodded in agreement on several points, but I assured her that there were very minor adjustments to be made. However, I told her that she had made a very fatal error in the early goings of the assessment. Susan could not grasp that possibility—she understood that she could have missed a few details, but none on the level of a fatal error. I asked her to think back, to think about the most important thing that has to happen during the assessment. She gave it a moment's thought, and it was then that her eyes betrayed her. She looked at me, and in her eyes I saw the lioness give way to the Eastern European girl who only wanted to know where to go, and how to get there. Her eyes had become those of a lost lamb.

I then asked her again: how do you feel? Before she could answer, I told her that the most important question she needs to ask a client is how they are feeling, and that the most significant data of the entire assessment process is the client's honest answer to that question. All the technical data that Susan had collected created a strong case for the client to start training, but it is the relative data, the data that helps us understand the story that the client brings with them, that creates the need for the relationship.

Susan looked away from me for a moment. She started to scribble a few notes, then very quickly stopped. She looked at me again, and she simply nodded and smiled. Susan wanted me to know how she felt. She wanted me to know that she understood. Her eyes and her smile confirmed that she would fulfill the promise I saw in her. She would achieve success as a personal trainer.

THE COMPONENTS OF THE ASSESSMENT

In an assessment, there are two types of data. I have used the descriptions of these categories from Daniel Kahnemann, an award-winning economist whose book *Thinking Fast and Slow*, should be on the bookshelf of every personal trainer.

1. **Relevant Data:** This is the category of information that measures baseline fitness. Aside from body composition and heart rate metrics, data that falls into this category includes medical, surgery, and injury history, along with sports that the client either participated in or is involved in. This is the kind of data also includes measurable and quantifiable information obtained from the instruments of our trade, such as heart rate monitors, body fat calipers, and scales. This data will determine your client's physical baseline.

2. **Relative Data:** This category, in essence, is the client's story that they would like to share with you. Note the phrase "that they would like to share." A person's story is their favored construct of

how they relate to the rest of the world. In other words, this is how they would like to be seen—this is how they would like YOU to see THEM.

How you reconcile the relevant data in your assessment (which is the result of your technical expertise in using your equipment) with the relative data that you have received from your client, will determine your ability to *connect* with your client. If you are successful, your assessment will have the backing of legitimate facts, combined with the emotional impact of intimately knowing their story—perhaps more than they had first anticipated. When you achieve this, you will have given them a presentation of your findings that will fully resonate with the client on a deeper level than they had initially anticipated. Your client will feel that you know them, and you are presenting data that is *relevant* to them.

The assessment must allow the trainer the opportunity to collect the relative and relevant data easily and efficiently. It should include:

1) **An intake form:** It should include at minimum several questions about medical, injury, and surgery history. It should be filled out by both the client and trainer, as it will begin establishing the partnering aspect of their relationship early on, and builds the necessary trust between you and your client. All this, and your client has yet to do a single exercise.

2) **Physiological tests:** Height, weight, heart rate, blood pressure, and body composition tests are necessary to establish not only your expertise, but are also bio-markers that you, as the fitness professional, will revisit to show that the client is making progress toward their fitness goals on the program that you designed for them.

3) **Movement assessment:** This is a must for all assessments because it opens up an opportunity for you to speak about program design and exercise selection in a far more authoritative manner, since movement quality is a relatively new component

of training that has yet to really penetrate the mainstream. It allows you to discuss myofascial lines, neural patterning, and how movement affects brain health—areas of potential interest to the client that will showcase your knowledge and expertise. The relevant data collected will also greatly inform the exercise selection and progression for this client, allowing the trainer to further customize the client's experience.

4) **Goals:** A discussion about fitness goals is a layered conversation that requires a sophisticated approach. The client's goals are based on a subjective understanding of themselves, and how they would like that perspective to change. When a client shares their goals with a trainer, they are ultimately revealing their hidden aspirations and vulnerabilities. A wish list of a 15-pound weight loss, more toned legs, and a 4-inch loss in waist size is part of the *relative* data collection process. For example, 15 pounds ago the client may have been in the best shape of their life, and they associate that time with happiness, vitality, and peak performance. A 4-inch waist loss may also indicate when they could fit better in their clothes, thereby feeling more presentable and confident when they are in a professional setting or a social environment. Being able to understand, deeply, the *relative* value of these metrics to the client (i.e. achieving them will help them feel more vital and happy) will not necessarily help you design a better program for them. However, it will help you *connect* with the client as someone who is willing to partner with them and ultimately lead them to success.

It is important for you to consider that during the process of implementing these components that you do not lose your desire to understand the potential client. Although the necessary data will help you in creating a highly-customized and effective program that can deliver the desired results, the process should always be about understanding the client better simply as a human being. What you will do, in effect, is to humanize a process that can, at times, be heavily laden in clinical technicalities and common jock-mentality. Make understanding your primary tool, and building a relationship your primary goal. By doing so, you will remain connected to the humanity of your client, as well as your own.

THE MACRO-CYCLE

There are some who believe that small, sustainable benchmarks for progression are considered "better" than making drastic changes in lifestyle and exercise choices that may deliver dramatic results, but with little sustainability and higher chance of health risks. Far too often a client will offer you goals that they deem realistic, for the purposes of ensuring an achievable level of success, with a minimum risk of failure.

Macro-cycle programming incorporates this approach within the framework of a strategy that requires a greater span of time, more financial and emotional investment, and a vision of total transformation. It may, at first, be beyond the potential client's imagination, and they may communicate their reservations about its achievability. This is not an immediate concern, because the communication of your long-term vision for your client reveals what *you believe* is within *their* realm of possibility and how invested you are in the process of training them because you believe in them. In other words, rather than teaching them how to walk, you are going to point them in the direction of a beautiful and clearly articulated vision of where they will be walking toward, and inspiring them to work towards this vision—full bore, self-directed, and self-managed.

It is fair to say that clients, by and large, need motivation to achieve the goals that they want, and to work consistently with the program that you have established. Most clients do not reach their goals simply because they lack the discipline to stick to the program, or the commitment to stick to it over the long term. However, if our *financial success* is dependent upon a substantial roster of clients who train consistently and achieve results, it is not within our best interests to believe that clients by *nature* lack the willpower to stick to a program.

It is common and even acceptable for fitness experts to believe that clients may be unmotivated, but for the trainer this is anathema to managing a business successfully. It places far too much of your business upon the whims of your clients, and not enough emphasis on examining what you, as a fitness professional and business owner, can do about solving this problem for yourself. Our profession could do a better of job of holding itself accountable to our ultimate success by simply believing that managing clients towards a broader, long-term, and more inspirational set of goals will drive them towards achieving those goals.

When people go on vacation, they will take on the stresses of traffic, airports, flights, and certain financial costs if the final destination is filled with the promise of good food, relaxation, a beautiful new environment, and the promise of adventure. In other words, people will essentially follow directions on a map that is taking them someplace *new* and *rewarding*.

The Macro-Cycle approach to programming addresses this aspect of human nature and our innate need for new experiences and adventures. It is a long-term plan that has a final destination for the client that thrills, excites, challenges, and promises to be arduous and difficult. In our business, the territory your clients are exploring are their own bodies, and the experiences they are seeking are the positive emotions that come with overcoming the challenges of getting in shape. The trainer who understands this will be able to utilize their technical expertise to design a program that ignites their clients' imagination, which will bring them to levels that are not necessarily within the construct of the clients' relative data paradigms, but goes far beyond their perceived limitations in order to take them to the fulfillment of their own potential. The only limitation for the trainer is their level of education (formal, autodidactic, or both) which determines how the program is put together. Once the program is formalized, the trainer can communicate the program not only from the position of its effectiveness, but how the journey towards the end-goal is in and of itself rewarding.

Now, consider a program that is designed without an end-goal in mind, but with a prescription of regular exercise that requires the client to come in roughly three times a week to address the fundamental basics of cardiovascular fitness, movement quality, and baseline force generation. All three components will be addressed which, should affect body composition, vitality, posture, and an overall sense of well-being. Such a program would increase its effectiveness exponentially should it be implemented in conjunction with a sound nutrition protocol. Theoretically this sounds like a wonderful plan, but it loses steam because it does not vividly describe an end goal that is specifically formulated to motivate the client. For some, a program that produces quantifiable results can be a thrill in and of itself, but without a journey and a partner it becomes uninspiring and clinical: people are not necessarily motivated by such rewards if they do not clearly create a direct and transformative impact on their lives that is beyond their current perception of reality.

Why should our programs be scientifically sound and have an exciting end in mind for the client? Of course you need your clients to be motivated—business as a discipline requires that you are accountable for your success, and that success is dependent upon the level of engagement of your clients. However, there is a deeper and far more pragmatic purpose for programming via the macro-cycle: because effective training, by and large, is at its core very difficult and painful. A client will simply not push through the most difficult sets of your program design if they are not fully invested in a vision of themselves that the program supports. Clients are motivated by a vision of themselves that they will have achieved by following your program. It is not enough that it works, it has to inspire and invigorate.

Implementing a macro-cycle allows you to set out the goals as necessary benchmarks. This clear delineation is necessary for both you and your client to understand, because each goal is not an end in and of itself: it is an achievement that *builds* on another goal and achievement. With this carefully designed plan in place, the client is able to see the grand picture of what they are fully investing themselves in. They are assured that you will accompany them on this journey towards this vision. Though at times it can prove difficult, your relationship with the client will motivate them to push through challenges and overcome setbacks. The success of the journey comes for a mutual investment in each other and in the process.

SUSAN RISING

At 1PM on a very busy Monday afternoon, Susan came to my office door. She had a pile of programs in her folder for all of her clients, and she wanted to review a few of them with me. By this time, Susan had become one of the top producers in my division, and a formidable personal trainer. She had the uncanny ability to pick out a perfect program for any given member on any given day. Her meticulousness had taken on new levels of proficiency, as she could now spot a potential client on the floor by simply looking at them. More impressively, she could talk to anyone. Her mastery of English had improved slightly, but her mastery of the language of listening was without question. Whether she was talking to a young woman starting a workout regimen or a senior executive at a law firm, she knew how to make them all feel at ease.

On that busy afternoon, Susan was not quite at ease. She needed my input on several programs she had created for her clients, and she was crunched for time. I told her to put her programs away, because I needed her to sit in on one of my conference calls. I could see that she was becoming impatient, but I assured her that this was for her benefit, and that the call would last about 30 minutes. She protested mildly, but she deferred to my request. As her manager, I was always grateful that Susan often listened to me, because now more than ever I needed her to listen.

The conference call was about three initiatives that were being piloted, and my division was one of several that had been picked to manage the initiatives. It had been suggested that the manager pick three separate lead trainers to handle them accordingly. After several questions and answers about timelines and procedures, the call ended. Without a moment's hesitation, Susan quickly reached for her programs. She had been waiting long enough, and it was now her turn to chat with me. She started with her most important client—a senior executive who was recovering from knee surgery, and he wanted to train 5 times a week so that he can return to playing golf. She was sorting through his assessment and programs when I gave her the news: I had picked her to manage all three initiatives for our division.

There are moments in one's life when a few words fall from our minds and into our mouths, then to the ears of others. Sometimes those words travel without the slightest regard for destination or meaning. However, during the most important moments of our lives, our words do not travel so lightly. During these times our words have more meaning, so their journey takes a slight detour—these words come first from the heart.

Upon hearing that I had picked her to manage all three initiatives, her eyes steadily lit up, and a smile grew across her beautiful face. She tilted her head and said to me:

"You have lost your mind."

Susan stood up and started pacing my office. These were not the words I had exactly predicted, but the approximation was close enough so that I was duly prepared. Susan could not believe that I had picked her to manage all three initiatives. She said that the workload would be unbearable. She said that she was a top-producing trainer who had little time as it was. Not only would she be inefficient at her newly assigned tasks, she felt that she had been hand-picked to fail. I assured her that this was not the case, that she had my complete confidence in her abilities, and that I felt she would not fail.

This seemed to raise more of her ire, and she drove the point home even more. She felt I lacked the sensitivity to her situation as a sole provider for her sister and her child, that she would be stretched too thin, that she would not have the energy to be a top-producing trainer, be a good sister, and succeed at all three initiatives. Being a top-producer and provider were the most taxing components of her life, that she had nothing more to give me, and that she felt confused by my request.

I asked her calmly to take a seat. She looked at me cautiously before making the decision to finally sit down. Susan sat at the chair, and rested her hands on her lap. She did not move when I spoke to her. I took this opportunity to finally tell her my true intentions: I told her that I needed her to give me more, because I wanted to promote her to become my assistant manager in the division. I wanted her to run the division with me. I said to her that it was always my intention to promote her to management, because she had the qualities of a good leader. She had poise and assuredness, compassion, determination, courage, and now that she had the ability to connect, she could use those qualities to support her fellow trainers towards their success. Most importantly, it would give her the stability and flexibility she needed to spend more time with her family abroad. I needed her to manage all three initiatives, so that my recommendation for her promotion would be supported by upper management, which would be backed primarily by her unsurpassed efforts. I also assured her that she did not have to take on all three initiatives, that it was her choice, that she did not have to take the opportunity, but that I felt that she was the best candidate for managing them.

Susan then told me that she just realized what I had been doing all along was to groom her for her greatest challenge, and her greatest opportunity. And for that reason alone, she would do it.

THE SESSION

With your assessment completed, you are ready to give the client their complimentary session. Now it is important to clearly communicate the benefits of the program, how it is based on sound scientific methodologies, and how this particular approach will best benefit them. Do not lose sight of this one thing: the client, at least during their first session, is simply trying to figure out what the first steps of their journey will be like. They are trying to see how challenging it will be, how beneficial it will be. Most importantly, they are trying to ascertain what it will be like to train with *you*.

As much as the client is concerned with how effective the program is, none of that will be readily and immediately discernable, especially during the first session. The client is trying to figure out if *you* are someone they want to see on a regular basis. As much as you are assessing them from a professional point of view, they are also assessing your value to their journey for this simple reason: *they are highly aware of other options.* Whether those options come in more affordable packages such as group fitness, media, or a competing trainer, savvy clients are aware that their investment must deliver a particular return that the other offerings cannot give them. As much as training is on their mind, they also want to know if you are a pleasant individual to be with.

The client will commit their resources to the training for as long as the trainers support them during the most difficult exercises in both mind and spirit. Your value to your client will become apparent when they are at their most vulnerable—when they are feeling weak or unmotivated. During the training session, the client is more interested in the relationship that the two of you have, because the program does not take into account how they are feeling and performing *that day*. Your client is looking to you for things outside of the effectiveness of the program. They will seek you out for encouragement before they seek you out for advice. They need you for motivation. Above all, they will need you for praise and acknowledgment when they have either met or exceeded the expectations of a phase in their plan.

In other words, the client does not just need you to be an expert or to be 100% right. They are looking for you to be *invested*—when they are tired, when they feel like quitting, when they feel like giving up. Your client wants you to believe that they can do it. An intelligently designed program cannot replace the personal investment that the trainer makes when they decide to make building the relationship the priority *above* getting the clients the results they are looking for. This particular decision, of course, does not mean that it is acceptable for the client to not get the results they are looking for. It means that getting results is the by-product of personal investment, not necessarily that of technical expertise. If you are invested in the success of your client, you will do your best to ensure that *every* aspect of their session meets a high standard.

It is this sense of investment that the client must feel from you during every training session. A sense of *care* must seem evident in the way the program has been designed, which takes into account not just the relevant data that the trainer collected during the assessment, but the relative data that is part of the client's overall story. If a client once enjoyed skiing, but recent knee surgery has prevented them from enjoying their favorite pastime, it would be prudent to add a drill into the complimentary session that addresses the need, or desire, of the client to reclaim overall knee health, while relating that to the client's skiing activities. How that affects the client's overall fitness progress is peripheral, because we are introducing it into a program to show that client that we are listening, and that we care about what is important to him. We are capable of making changes in the program, because it is a shared investment in a journey that both have undertaken.

This also adds another dimension to the program by allowing the client a substantial amount of ownership over its content. This increased level of ownership allows the client to feel empowered in their journey, which is an invaluable asset because it makes the sometimes difficult interaction of motivating an unmotivated client easier. When a client starts to see results, when they believe they are progressing, their elation does not come from the validation of your program (that is your achievement, not theirs), but rather from a sense of regaining *control* over their essential experience. You are giving them a sense of being able to manage themselves, and it validates their ability to make the right choice and to control the nature of their experiences.

THE LIONESS IN WINTER

At 4AM in the morning, I received a call from Susan to ask me for a particular report that she needed for her conference call. At the time, I was vacationing in Honolulu, so the 4AM call was appropriate because it gave her time to prepare for her first conference call as a manager. When I took her call, she cheerfully said, "Good morning boss, how's the sunrise?"

Susan, at this point, had mastered The Four Competencies method to such a degree that not only had she successfully mentored several trainers in our division, she was also brimming with confidence. The promotion suited her well, as it brought about a calm but authoritative bearing to her already impressive poise. It was hard to tell that this was her first month as a manager, and with me on vacation she was at the helm and completely in charge.

After helping her locate a report, I quizzed her very briefly on the status of our team and our division's current performance metrics. It was the middle of January, so it was important that the team had high-morale to take advantage of members' New Year's Resolutions, and to also manage any potential problems that could affect the division's performance. Historical analysis showed that a good January tended to create the momentum necessary for a good-performing year, so January metrics needed to be approached carefully but also with a good dose of calmness.

Susan answered my questions with such clarity and confidence that I knew my division was in good hands. More importantly, I knew her growth as a manager was off to a good start. We joked a bit about a couple of my surfing and snorkeling exploits, before she asked me, "Are you tracking this blizzard that is supposed to hit the East Coast?" I confessed to her that I had not—I was in Honolulu with beautiful sunsets and beautiful waves. She laughed and said, "I will see you soon."

It turned out that the blizzard dumped 14 inches of snow in Manhattan. It had the obvious effect of throwing off transportation for members, which amounted to several late cancellations for sessions. We had prepared for this, so we were still on pace to perform and hit our goals. What we did not prepare for was that I would be stuck in Honolulu for another week—so Susan would be at the helm without me for much longer than she had anticipated.

On the eve of the blizzard, Susan called me at our usual 4AM time. This time, there was the slightest hint of concern in her voice. She wanted to discuss potential tactical switches, should the blizzard have more of a cascading effect on our division's performance. I told her that her concerns were valid, and that it was astute of her to want to discuss possible scenarios. I asked, "What are those potential scenarios?"

She listed them with precision. New clients may postpone their purchases in January to February, returning clients may have their travel plans affected by the blizzard, moving their scheduled sessions to February as well. Trainers may become demoralized, especially the new ones, who were fighting for every session and conversion. Susan knew the potential outcomes of each one, and I communicated to her that she had a very firm grasp of the business. Regardless of the outcome, her ability to understand potential threats to performance meant that she had grown substantially into her new role.

She laughed momentarily, then sighed. I asked her what the sigh was for. Her answer surprised me, but also gave me greater comfort that she knew what she was doing.

"I now understand what it is like to be in your shoes, to be head of division. In the face of potential success or failure, you are at the helm no matter what. No one has to know what you're feeling or thinking, you just have to be the one that takes care of everything. And I sighed because I know, someday, I won't have you as my mentor. I will have to do it on my own."

And she did exactly that, and masterfully so. My travel was delayed so that I arrived on the very last day of January. I had no reason to worry, because Susan had kept me in the loop through every step of her management decisions. By the time I had arrived at the office the next day, Susan had posted the best January performance in our division's history, despite the blizzard, despite my absence, and in her rookie month. Susan was still taking English language classes for further proficiency, but she had mastered her new role decisively. In the troublesome winter of January, a lioness walked the snowy landscape alone, undisturbed, and triumphant.

NOTES FOR THE AUTODIDACT

As your skills evolve, you will need to educate yourself in order to continue your growth. An autodidact, even one with an impressive capacity for growth through self-education and reflection, must be careful in how he attains this knowledge. Specifically, it is important to recognize within yourself knowledge that you have reached a particular proficiency in, as opposed to knowledge that you have yet to explore. Although our passion drives much of who we are as fitness professionals, we must temper it with a careful inventory of our existing knowledge, with a keen eye towards measuring our effectiveness. That effectiveness can be measured by how capable we are in connecting with our clients and understanding their journey. Knowledge, in and of itself, is not power, especially if that knowledge removes your ability to connect.

With this in mind, your continued education must be specific to improving your ability to connect with your clients. The value of a workshop or certification is measured by how the knowledge being offered allows you to understand your client's *journey, their goals, and their challenges on a _human level_*. This is what will make you better at your profession, and improve your expertise. If you cannot apply your knowledge to your client's experience, no matter how deeply researched and scientifically supported it is, that knowledge is useless. Any knowledge that makes you disconnect from your client's experience will make your client feel abandoned in their journey with you, regardless of how scientifically validated that knowledge may be. Your level of expertise is measured by how carefully you lead your client along their journey, with knowledge that brings you both to a greater understanding of what it is to be human.

Should you find yourself acquiring knowledge that puts you in the position of judging your client in any way, know that you have essentially compromised your ability to train them, because you now doubt their ability to succeed. When you are no longer capable of believing in your client's ability and willingness to achieve their goals, you have compromised your own ability to train them. When you no longer believe in your client, you are no longer the best person to get them to their goals.

Believe in them the way they need you to believe in them. The effectiveness of your expertise is limited only by the level of your commitment to your client's success. Never forget this.

THE SECOND COMPETENCY

CUSTOMER CARE

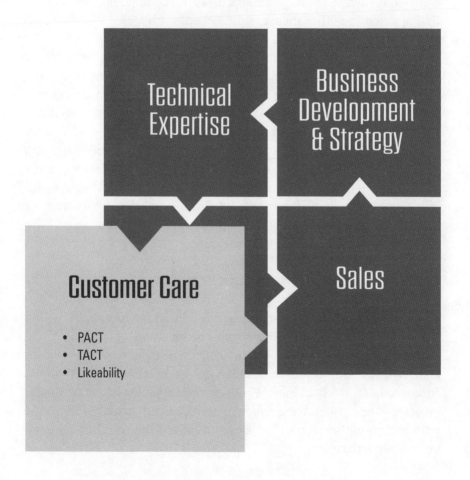

Technical Expertise

Business Development & Strategy

Customer Care

- PACT
- TACT
- Likeability

Sales

Connecting with your client as a person will determine the overall experience not just for them, but also for you; it gives you the opportunity to establish a relationship outside of your role as an expert. Your belief in your client's ability to achieve their goals is paramount to you being able to train them. Your technical expertise will be compromised if you do not believe in your client's ability to succeed. If you are to accept that your role in the lives of our members is to be the leader in their fitness journey, you must accept that leading through personal connection is your primary mode of operation.

For this reason alone, customer care is often the most difficult competency for trainers to implement, particularly for those who are completely invested in the technical expertise competency, and believe that this alone qualifies them to train a client.

In many ways, the difficulty is understandable because these trainers have been conditioned to view clients from a single perspective: are they or are they not in shape? They perceive their value to the client is connected to whether what the client needs is in essence, a product that can be purchased and that they, the fitness expert, can give them from a position of authority. This is an important detail to understand, and requires deep reflection because what often makes more trainers avoid an interaction that requires customer care is that it removes the badge of authority that makes their word definitive and final. You must be careful that your expertise does not prevent you from connecting with clients whose lives you are hoping to change.

From the perspective of effective leadership, customer care is the competency that enhances your ability to connect with your client on more level ground. Most trainers would prefer to operate within the trainer/client relationship from the position of expertise and authority—by being the expert in their chosen field, their opinions and insights are usually unchallenged because the client is not educated in exercise science. When a trainer explains how a particular myofascial line affects a movement pattern, a client usually accepts the information without question, simply because the terminology is so unfamiliar to the client.

While this does create a level of partnership between trainer and client, it does not necessarily achieve the level of connectedness between the two of them that only inspirational leadership can produce. Your client may believe in you, but in order for them to succeed, you have to lead them to believe in themselves. Leadership can be an effective and indirect mode of teaching, without making the client aware that they are being expertly guided and educated.

There is also a subtle line of thinking that we must address before proceeding with the P.A.C.T./T.A.C.T. customer care model for the 4C Method. When trainers think of gym members, they often make the assumption that the member is:

- Out of shape
- Unmotivated
- Lazy
- Vain
- Uneducated in exercise science and nutrition
- Unskilled
- Weak
- Undisciplined
- Fat

Admit it: at one point or another, you thought this way about gym members in general, and some of your clients in particular. Some still think this way. In many ways, there is a grain of truth in this line of thinking. Let us set aside the possibility that even one of these descriptions accurately depicts your member base, or any of your existing clients. I'm not saying that this may not often be true, but let me ask you a simple question: *how can you help someone if you think of them in a negative light?*

Let's look at a common scenario we find in the gym:

We are on the gym floor, observing members working out. One individual is on the treadmill, sprinting at an elevated incline. He seems to be running for his life, and is gasping for breath. He leans on the handles, which gives him a break. Then he lets go of the handles, going on a full sprint again. He presses the emergency stop button, bringing the treadmill to a halt, and he gasps for breath.

Now he gets down on the floor, a sopping mess of perspiration. He proceeds to do a set of pushups, bodyweight squats, and leg lifts—all executed with poor form. The pushups are done with a collapsed lower back, squats are done only a quarter of the way down, and the legs barely leave the floor on the concentric portion of the exercise.

There are two ways to approach this member, with the possibility of turning them into a client.

1) The Helpful Expert: this trainer desires to help correct the member's approach to exercise. She sees the member's breathing patterns need to be corrected, and offers assistance to help him be more efficient. She can give the member pointers about the treadmill, or suggest that he slow down. Perhaps she gives him a little advice about determining target-heart rates, along with some helpful tips on form for pushups and leg lifts to make them safer.

2) The Contemptuous Expert: in the end, this trainer will also help the member, and give similar pieces of advice. However, in the back of her mind this trainer will not be able to help themselves from criticizing and judging the member. In fact, more often than not, she will be judging the member *as* she is helping him.

Perhaps there is something to be said about the fact that one expert is trying to be helpful, while the other is contemptuous. One is offering tips on exercise hoping that the client benefits from their advice, while the other does the same with a somewhat similar sense of superiority. We have, in our careers as fitness professionals, at one time or another, held the mindset of both trainers, convincing ourselves that we are trying to be helpful, that we are doing our jobs.

Let us do this from a slightly different perspective: the perspective of the member.

The member is in his late 20's and a former lacrosse player. He got into finance because of pressure from his parents, when in fact he wanted to be an artist. Just a few months ago, his father passed away from a sudden heart attack. Just a few weeks ago, his girlfriend of 2 years broke up with him because he wasn't managing his health. He reasoned that work was taking up so much of his life that it didn't afford him the luxury of training the way he used to.

He hurt his back over a year ago while snowboarding with his girlfriend's family, which ruined the family vacation.

He recently got his annual review, and his performance for the prior year was mediocre at best. He was advised by his manager to join a gym, to manage his health and stress levels better.

The question we must ask ourselves is this—*how does this client see himself?* Does the client see himself as "treadmill/goofy pushup guy", or as someone who needs a little bit of help and luck to turn things around? This individual just:

- Lost their father
- Lost their girlfriend
- Is unfit and most likely unhealthy
- Is in pain from their injury
- Is at risk of losing their job

If we go back to our previous list, this member already feels:

- Out of shape
- Unmotivated
- Unappreciated
- Isolated

In light of this scenario, we must ask ourselves a very important question: if the member already feels this way, *are we being helpful by reinforcing what they are feeling?* The answer is a resounding *no.*

Consider, also, the alternatives that this member had other than come in and work out:

- Stay home
- Go out to socialize
- Drink excessively
- Eat excessively

With this new information we have a different perspective:

Despite not being as athletic as he used to be because of an injury, despite losing two people he loves, despite being on the verge of losing his job, despite the lack of support in his life, this individual chose (among the many unhealthy activities he could have chosen to participate in), to join a gym to workout to the *best of his current abilities.*

There are a few things to consider:

- If you feel even the slightest amount of contempt or judgment for a client, potential or actual, you are not in the best position to help them, *regardless of your level of expertise and education.*

- If you feel that the most important thing that your client needs is your *expertise and education,* you are also not in the best position to help this person.

I hope it is now clear that technical expertise, in this scenario (which is rather common), has its initial limitations. First, your expertise will blind you to what someone may be going through outside of the context of training. Second, your expertise creates a narrow focus that does not allow you to see the whole individual—all you will see is whether or not this individual *fits your paradigm and definition of fitness and excellence.* And last, your expertise loses its value as a tool for helping people; it becomes a barrier to entry for building real relationships that are ultimately important to your growth as a mature individual. No amount of expertise or competency is valuable if it prevents you from relating authentically with other human beings in a way that allows for compassion and understanding. Knowledge is supposed to bring people together, not pull them apart.

It is in this light that customer care comes to the fore. When it comes to building an authentic relationship with your members and clients—you must let go of your pride in your gilded certificates and your expertise and come from a place of genuine emotional warmth. You must not look upon your members from a place of superiority, but rather from a place of respect and equality. You must remember that you were also, at one point in your development, goofy, awkward, eager, but desperate, and needed the help and guidance of someone who cared about your growth and success.

Your members and clients do not need your expertise. They need you to believe in them first. And this starts with praise— your opportunity to connect with your client on this level starts by relinquishing your technical expertise, and by approaching the client from the position of customer care.

HAL

I met Hal when I was just starting my career as a manager. It was early in the spring in NYC, and his interview was scheduled on a bright beautiful day. Usually, springtime in New York is met with a healthy dose of skepticism, for such beautiful days are often (and without warning) followed by dark and cold rainy nights that often turn to treacherous ice. Year after year, New Yorkers bemoan the seeming unpredictability of our weather conditions, despite the fact that they tend to follow the same uncooperative and non-linear pattern. Predicting the weather is to a certain extent scientific, but predicting New York weather is best left to the meteorological equivalent of shamans.

That day I approached the front desk and was introduced to Hal, a young man of African-American descent in his early 20's. He met me with a bright smile and a firm handshake. He was well-dressed and well-groomed, trim and tall, he greeted me by saying, "Thank you sir for the opportunity to interview for your division."

Hal had been pre-screened by Susan, and since I trusted her word on her selection of applicants, I did not bother to look at his resume. His bearing and presentation alone convinced me that this young man was capable of connecting immediately with our member-base purely on his well-mannered approach. As I escorted him to the office, I noticed how cheerful he seemed. He had an easy manner to him, as if he was not about to be interviewed, but instead he acted as if he was about to make a new friend.

We had an opportunity to sit-down and discuss his reasons to become a personal trainer. He spoke passionately about his desire to become a professional trainer, to join a team that offered great support and encouragement, and that he wanted nothing more than to be able to fulfill his potential in this, his chosen field.

I nodded and smiled at this young man, and asked for his resume. He reached into his sport jacket to pull out his resume. I thought the gesture odd—where was his portfolio? I thanked him for giving me his resume. When I unfolded the piece of paper, I noticed immediately how unpopulated it was with the typical things one sees in a professional resume. He had no certificates, no advanced degrees, no experience to speak of in the realm of personal training. His education consisted of a few semesters at a community college, and that his last professional post was that of a concierge at a luxury condominium in New Jersey.

I asked him if he was currently employed. He hesitated, and for a moment I saw in this young man's face the first sign of uncertainty. He said to me, "I am currently a limo driver."

I then asked him if he had ever trained anyone. This time without hesitating, but quietly he answered, "No."

Hal looked at the door, as if to anticipate what my next words would be. In all honesty, I had no words to say to him, because there was absolutely nothing in his resume that would in any way recommend him as a personal trainer, let alone as a member of my team. He then looked at me and he said, "I am from the Bronx. I don't have an education. I don't come from much. I just want a chance for something better, and I love fitness. I know I don't have the goods, but if you hire me, I promise you I will give it my best shot. I won't let you down."

I said to Hal, "If you can make good on that promise, you will become a very good trainer and you can be a part of my team. But you have to make good on it. And you have to pass the second round of interviews—which includes both of my superiors. They can be very critical. Are you really game for this?"

Hal leaned a little closer to me, and gave me a look that only a friend would give another friend. It is the kind of look that you get from a friend who wants to assure you that he is in it with you, to let the dice fall where they may, because wherever the journey takes the two of you, you are both in it together. Hal then smiled as brightly as a spring day, and said simply: "I'm game."

P.A.C.T.—PRAISE, ASSIST, COACH, TEACH

If you put yourself in the shoes of the former lacrosse player, you will understand that the last thing that man needs is a super-fit, good-looking trainer telling him that he is doing everything wrong. He has enough reminders in his life that he could be doing things better. One could ask, in this instance, "Then why are you in the gym if you are not here to get better?" The answer is simple: our members and clients are looking for inspiration. Inspiration doesn't start with finding what is wrong—it starts with *finding what is right.*

Your relationship with your potential client starts with observing what they are doing right, which is the foundation of praise. By finding positive, praise-worthy aspects of this member's behavior you separate yourself from other trainers, and possibly other people in your clients life; you may be, perhaps the ONLY person in their lives who gives them any sort of praise. This fact alone—not your expertise—gives your role tremendous value simply because you are the one who honestly sees value in them. In other words, you are the one person who sees that what they are doing counts toward *something*.

Now, the question is: "What *can* I praise about this member?" Here is a short list of possibilities:

- They are running on the treadmill at a high-speed *and* on an incline
- They are combining endurance exercises with bodyweight training, which is a form of cross-training
- They are working up a sweat
- They seem determined
- They are in the gym working out

These are 5 *genuine* observations about this member that are not only praise-worthy, but something that the member will greatly appreciate simply because you made the observation and made the effort to communicate it. Most importantly, you will be coming from a place of authenticity because you took the time to *classify* your observations into two categories:

- Strengths
- Areas of Development

Most trainers will often observe a potential client and communicate areas of possible development first, mistaking it as their primary area of opportunity. Your true area of opportunity is to observe obvious strengths, and communicate them to the member, making them aware of what they can leverage during their training. This is the essential mechanism of praise—communicate the strengths of the individual, so that they can leverage them during their workouts.

There is an important difference between praising a member versus "staying positive"—a form of praise that is based on generalities, as opposed to specifically observed attributes and actions. The former is a form of data collection, as you will be using these observations throughout your ongoing relationship with them. When you praise someone's strengths, you inspire them to rely on those strengths when the going gets tough, not just in their sessions with you, but in their life in general. Most importantly, you are communicating to the client that you are, in fact, paying close attention to everything that they do, and that you are using your observations to help them achieve their goals.

Customer care, in essence, is an *extension* of our technical expertise, because it allows us to utilize our powers of observation in a context that empowers the individual. The technical expertise skill-set allows us to validate the integrity of our product and our approach. Each observation helps create powerful and specific sessions and programs. The customer care skill-set allows us to affirm our clients' concerns and efforts, giving them validity and value. This combination of customized program while leveraging the strengths that the client brings to the table ultimately defines the value of what we do. We are, perhaps, the *only* professionals who manage both the physical and psychological needs of the clients who are in our charge. This is what makes our role significant.

The next step in the process is to assist the member in whatever they happen to be doing. This is important, because at this point most eager trainers will default to being an expert (in one form or another), and start correcting the member. This does not mean we should not be correcting our member—it simply means we have to wait, because there are two other very important steps that need to be established first.

Praising the member, then offering to assist them as their partner establishes the two very important components to the future of your relationship with them:

- Your partnership will always be about their strengths and how to make them highly effective at using them.
- Their journey is self-determined, and you are there to help and partner with them in that journey.

This is the quintessential win-win proposition: Your communication will be centered around how to best develop and utilize the member's existing strengths to make the journey and partnership as beneficial for both you and the client.

Consider the alternatives:

- You are there to make them aware of weaknesses they are already highly aware of.
- You are reminding them that they are not performing well, and you will determine the course of their journey.

The above is a zero-sum proposition: you are the expert, and the client is there to simply be educated by you. You are there to dole out advice and training, and they are there to simply listen to you, if they want to achieve the results they want.

All things being equal, the 4C Method has found that members generally prefer the praise/assist approach for this simple reason: if a member is going to pay $200 an hour (or $50 or $75 an hour) 3 times a week (or once a week) to be trained by an effective professional, they would rather spend their *time with someone who praises them and partners with them*, rather than with an expert who does not praise and comes exclusively from a place of authority. Members prefer to see their trainers as their *partners*—they have enough "experts" in their lives telling them what to do and what not to do.

In this case, assisting a member means that you will forego correcting their form for now. You will instead offer:

- Counting reps
- Getting them a towel or a bottle of water
- Setting up the treadmill

By approaching them with the mindset of partnering as opposed to educating, you are helping them with *their* workout and have created a positive interaction with a member who is already receiving value from the relationship—without you once mentioning your multiple certifications or the price structure of your fees.

Praise, combined with assistance and correction, is how every session between a trainer and client should go. *Now* you can start coaching the member on their form and execution. By praising, assisting, then correcting the client—in that order—during this initial interaction, you have given them a preview of how it will be to train with you, and how each session can be this fun and engaging.

Coming back to our former lacrosse athlete, now is the time to:

- Remind them to keep their back straight during a pushup via cueing.
- Show them the most effective form for a squat.
- Illustrate the necessary range of motion for effective leg lifts.

When you praise your client and offer to assist them *first*, they will be more open to receiving your corrections. You have positioned yourself as someone who is offering compassionate support and understands their individual needs, as opposed to you giving them a set of expectations by which they will be judged. Everyone is looking for someone to join them in their journey, to share in their exploits and challenges. People do not listen to experts; they listen to people who care about them. People do not listen to experts who make them feel bad, regardless of how sound and relevant the advice is. They listen to people who are willing to listen to them. Members are not in the gym just to get results. They are looking for inspiration in their lives, to see that they are capable of making a difference. No amount of expertise or measurable results will inspire a member to believe in themselves the way they need to—only a trainer who has the skill to lead and be compassionate can serve to be the guiding force that can transform a person's life in a way that is relevant and has a lasting impact.

Once you have praised, assisted, and corrected this member, now is the opportune time to teach them about what they have just *experienced*. Take careful note: we are teaching them about what they have *immediately* experienced, as opposed to the virtues of exercise, good nutrition, and a good night's rest because that is what the member is ready to hear about. Address what they are experiencing in their current reality. When you have coached them through proper pushup form, teach them about the corrections you gave them. More importantly, teach them *regressions* and *progressions* related to that exercise. This will help you connect your expertise to their *experience*, educating them on what they perceive as their current need, as opposed to offering advice on a reality that they have yet to become aware of. Always approach your communication with your client from the perspective of what they are experiencing in the moment, so you can find a way to connect your knowledge to who they are and what they are feeling. This is why knowledge by itself is useless in engaging a client: if it does not connect to their immediate concerns, it is useless to them. It is also useless to you, in terms of managing your business.

The Praise/Assist/Coach/Teach Method—P.A.C.T. for short, puts you in a position that goes beyond your ability to train a particular client:

- You have positioned yourself as a primary source of praise in this person's life. If they become your client, this praise will come regularly on a twice to three times a week basis.
- You have also positioned yourself as a partner in their journey towards developing themselves. You offer guidance and advice while they make decisions and hold themselves accountable.
- You are correcting them in their exercises and their workouts, offering efficiency and insight, but from the position of being their positive partner.
- You are capable of utilizing your expertise within the context of the member's experience in a way that can be valued immediately.

If you have accomplished these four things, you have essentially given them a sneak-peak of what it will be like to train with you and have established a relationship that is founded on mutual trust, partnership, and inspiration—*before* the member has agreed to purchase any training sessions with you or before you have offered them an assessment or complimentary session. Perhaps this is outside your job description as a personal trainer, but it is—and should be—the nature of the role you will fulfill in the lives of your members and future clients.

In fact, you can utilize the P.A.C.T. method not just with this member, but with every member you come across. Imagine that your day is filled with these positive interactions:

- You will be praising and assisting everyone you interact with in the gym on a daily basis.
- You will be viewed by members and clients as someone very positive and helpful.
- You are training yourself to closely observe the positive aspects of every individual you come across.

Think very carefully of the 3 things that P.A.C.T. can do for you, beyond the ability to possibly get a member to purchase sessions and train with you. You are essentially training your observational skills to look *specifically for strengths in each individual you interact with*. This alone makes you very valuable because most people are only capable of observing flaws and weaknesses in others. Though this has a certain value, most people are not inspired by making them aware of their weaknesses, because they are already very aware of their weaknesses— you add little value to their lives by being another voice that points out the obvious, the redundant, and the uninspiring. However, most people are not aware of their strengths, and you add value to your relationship with them by pointing out what they have either not observed or are not capable of leveraging. This applies not just to members, but to everyone you interact with.

By observing their strengths, you have positioned yourself as a source of inspiration, positive energy, and encouragement when they are down and discouraged. Your ability to assist them is dependent upon their perception of you as someone who sees the best in people and has the ability to give them guidance on how to become better at whatever it is they are doing.

This approach is one that benefits *everyone*, especially you because it gives you the ability to showcase your value outside of your ability to help someone lose weight or get stronger. It is here that the trainer starts to understand that the role of leadership is part and parcel of being a fitness professional.

A PORTRAIT OF THE TRAINER
AS A YOUNG MAN

My two superiors brought me into their office to discuss my new trainer Hal. Specifically they wanted to discuss his current progress, so they asked me to put together his reports and current standing with the team. When I knocked on the door, my superiors were seated at the end of the conference room table. They stood up and welcomed me, only to sit back down immediately. They said it would be a quick meeting.

They asked how my division was doing, and I replied that it was in good shape. The team had more top producers on hand, client count was up, and overall performance and morale were at an all-time high. They replied that they were elated with the division's performance. They had been observing on the floor how happy our members were with their training. Trainers in particular, even the old-timers, felt that these were the glory days of the division. They congratulated me heartily and sincerely.

But with the same sincerity, they expressed their concern for my new trainer, Hal. Before I could manage their feedback, they asked for my folder, which contained Hal's progress reports. I walked over to where they were sitting, and quickly turned around to get back to my seat, hoping I could be back in my seat to explain to them how Hal was actually progressing before they perused the papers. I heard one of them rifling through the papers, slowly and deliberately. My other superior did not bother with the reports—he spoke plainly, as I raced to my chair.

"We are concerned about Hal. He has been with the team for some time now, and he is very well liked by the team and the members. Our concern is that he may be too focused on being well liked, but not enough on getting members to sign up with him. Do you see where we are coming from?"

I explained that not everyone progresses at the same rate. Some trainers are late bloomers, because they take their time to build those relationships. I also explained that the reports are, admittedly, not favorable in terms of measuring performance, but I also explained that on the floor he is making many friends, and that I had faith that he simply needed time to turn them into clients.

My other superior was still rifling through Hal's report when he started speaking. "Have you thought about what would happen to him, if he does not have enough clients? He will have to quit this job, because he won't be able to make a living at this. There is more at stake here—a lot of people would be disappointed to see him go. I, for one, do not want to see him go. I want to see him succeed, like his colleagues. I think they all do. The team wouldn't be the same without him. Can you imagine your gym floor without him? We all need your help here. Can you help him?"

I fell silent. Hal had extraordinary energy, and the very idea of him not being on the floor, cheering everyone on, making people feel good just for being there...I understood more clearly in that moment what he was bringing to the team. I made my decision to bring some urgency and awareness to what he needed to do.

"Hal has to do it, we know he can do it. Not everyone you hire becomes a superstar, but when you hire one, make sure they live up to their end of the bargain and become one. We know he will be in later today. We'll let you handle it."

Later that day, I brought Hal into the office. He seemed cheerful as usual, but he had also heard from his friends that I had come from a tough meeting, and that the meeting was about him.

The door closed behind him, and he took his seat. He asked me how I was doing, and I was plain with him.

"Hal, you're a superstar. We all think you're a superstar, but you're not there yet. I need you to do this for you, because I can't. You have to want this for you, because I can't. Your team can't, your clients can't. Only you can do this for you."

He tensed visibly after hearing that, and understandably so. He acknowledged that his performance was not where either of us wanted it to be. He also acknowledged that he knew he needed to hear this. He said that he received his certification results today, and that he was finally certified as a trainer. He had also signed up for courses in movement analysis and advanced nutrition.

I asked him his score on the certification test. He answered "95%".

I was impressed, but I couldn't show him that yet. He needed more than a 95% score on a test. He needed more than technical expertise and a friendly demeanor.

"Hal, you need 12 clients in the next two months. Can you do it?"

"Yes. 100%", he replied.

"Then do it", I said.

To which he replied "I can do it. For me, for you, for everyone. Thank you, my liege."

"My liege? Where did you get that?"

"Hotspur from Shakespeare's Henry IV, Part I. Someone told me that you had classical training and that this was one of your favorite speeches. 'My liege, I did deny no prisoners...' I read it. In fact, the character Hal goes on to become King Henry The Fifth, right?"

"Yes," I replied, shocked at his sudden ability to reference classical theater, let alone my favorite speech. "That speech was filled with defiance, but he did it so intelligently, so good with words. But Hal, he gives up what he loves, even his best friends, in order to become a king. The leader of..."

"'This poor seat of England'", Hal answers. "That's what he says to the messenger when he becomes King, and he stands up for himself, his kingdom, and his claim. Yes, that was sad when he gave up the things and people he had previously loved. But he understood things differently. He understood what would happen if he did not stand up, if he did not make those sacrifices. What else did he say? He said...'We few, we happy few, we band of brothers...' When I read that speech, it reminded me of our team. It also reminded me of you. How you always inspire us. How you always inspire me."

Before I could say anything to Hal, he looks at me, then says, "I take my leave of you, my liege."

With that, he stood up, smiled, shook my hand, and left my office. He won. I knew he would win.

T.A.C.T.—THANK, ACKNOWLEDGE, CHALLENGE, THUMBS-UP

I once had the opportunity to train with a renowned martial arts master while on vacation. When I arrived to the master's class, he walked across the mats to me and said, "Thank you for coming to my class."

I was taken by surprise, and I asked him why he had thanked me. His response embodies the heart of the P.A.C.T. and T.A.C.T. methodology of customer care:

"I am thanking you because you made time to come to my class while you are on vacation. You could have chosen to go hiking, swimming, relaxing, drinking, or partying, but instead you made time to honor my class with your dedication and your commitment to your training. I am honored that you are here. Thank you for coming."

Always be aware, first and foremost, that your client chose to train with you. They could have trained with other trainers, they could have taken a group fitness class, or they could have decided to socialize and skip the gym altogether. They chose to spend their time with you.

Second, they chose to spend their money on your services. They could have chosen to spend that on another trainer, another service, or dinner with their friends. The point is that you must be clear that your livelihood is dependent upon your ability to persuade a client that they need your product and services. Regardless of your skills of persuasion and level of expertise, the final decision to purchase sessions with you on a regular and consistent basis rests solely upon the client. That decision, at the end of the day, is based on the relationship that you have established, which is built on mutual trust and partnership. They have decided to entrust their time, money, and effort in your abilities; in return, you must thank them for their dedication and their trust in the *partnership*.

If you examine this concept more closely, you will come again to the simple idea that on the gym floor there is little observable difference between a trainer who has an advanced level of education as opposed to another with less training and certification. What is very obvious is the level of dedication and commitment the *client* is displaying during their session with their trainer. That is determined less by the level of expertise that the trainer brings to their session, but more by the kind of partnership that both trainer and client have established. As much as this partnership has been established via the P.A.C.T. method, it is further deepened and developed by the T.A.C.T. method.

The T.A.C.T method is best employed when you already have a working relationship with the client, and they are training with you on a regular basis. At first glance, it may seem redundant to apply customer care to a client who is already training with you. This particular line of thinking presumes that since the client has already bought in to the program and your services, the best way to guarantee that they will continue to train with you is to ensure that the program is sound and that it delivers measurable results: if the client's fitness level is improving, that is the only customer care they will need. If we assume this, we are ignoring a very important driver of success—the client's individual level of dedication and their personal work ethic. If we were in the business of prescribing pills and the client achieved their goals based on regular administration of the pill we have prescribed, we can take the majority of credit for them achieving their goals.

This is not the case in personal training, because at the end of the day it is the client who is actually training. The client must choose to be dedicated to their training, choose to listen to your guidance, and choose to believe in themselves in order to reap the benefits of your partnership. Without this level of dedication, not only will they not achieve their results, the partnership will have proven to be ineffective, regardless of the effectiveness of your carefully designed training program that (on paper) should have worked—if only that client had "listened" to you. In this light, it is important for us as trainers to admit to ourselves that this partnership is necessary to achieve the client's goals, because it is within both your interests that this is achieved.

Without recognizing this, you run the risk of losing your client. You may say to yourself that you can always get another client. What will cause harm to you, however, is if the client chooses to train with someone else, and achieves their goals when they could not with you. When that occurs, their assumption will be that your expertise was lacking—regardless of the fact that you are very capable and your program very effective. The damage has been done.

Once you recognize that the effectiveness of your training program is, by and large, directly affected by the level of your client's dedication and adhere to that program, it is your duty to acknowledge that level of dedication and effort—and reinforce it during every session. When you are both done with the session, it is important to thank the client for their effort. We thank the client for showing up, for not giving up, for giving it their best, for believing in your abilities and in themselves. This gives the client a sense of recognition that, in reality, rarely occurs. This is an important component of your relationship, because most people are not recognized for their best efforts at home, at work, and in their daily lives. In fact, what requires the most recognition are the daily and consistent efforts without which everyone's lives would be diminished.

No one thanks the worker who stays an extra hour at work because he wants to make sure that report is perfect; often he is berated for poor time management. The same worker is scolded by his spouse when he comes home late; she feels he is neglecting his family. That same worker is staying an extra hour *because* they are dedicated to their professional duties, to the benefit of the company. That same worker is staying also to ensure the job security that his family benefits from. If this individual is not recognized for his specific effort, he will be less engaged simply because his efforts are rewarded with negative consequences, although they are positively contributing to the stability and growth of both company and family.

In this context, the significance of thanking a client for their dedication and efforts becomes clear. When put in the context of what is essentially a societal dilemma—trainers are perhaps the *only* people who are open and generous with their praise and assistance by thanking their clients for their specific dedication to their training. Our influence goes beyond the program we are offering—we are capable of making our clients feel that they are important, and that their efforts count for something worthwhile. Thank them for bringing their best to every session. Thank them for their dedication, then acknowledge them for what they did. Acknowledge them for the specific *performance-related* efforts that they displayed during the session; it shows that they are getting what they paid for—you are paying close attention to their training, particularly the qualitative aspects of their movement. If a client completes a series of pull-ups, acknowledge the form that they displayed. If their form was not perfect, acknowledge the degree of difficulty that they experienced, but that it was important for them to complete it regardless. If they did not complete the series, acknowledge that the exercise was very difficult, but that their efforts are nonetheless valuable towards their goals.

Acknowledging both the qualitative and quantitative aspects of your client's efforts displays the degree and intensity of observation that you give to every session, which matches their dedication and their commitment. When you are thanking and acknowledging their efforts and their performances, you are further reinforcing your own commitment to the partnership that you have both established. You are in it *with* them, you are training *alongside* them, you share in their victories and cushion their setbacks, you cheer them on, you advise them when they are going down a harmful path, yet empower them with the ability to choose—these are all tools that are within your beck and call as a fitness professional but only become apparent when you see yourself as a partner in their journey.

By designing a macrocycle for your clients you can clearly show them where they started, how far they have come, what obstacles they have put behind them, and how much closer they are to where they are going. Your technical expertise as expressed through effective management of periodization becomes most apparent when it is delivered within the context of partnership and intelligently crafted customer care. Technical expertise and customer care, working together, is the definition of professionalism in personal training.

On the client's end, they start to see several things fall into place. Not only do they have the dedication to train consistently, they have the ability to achieve their goals on a progressive and systematic scale. It also shows that they were *right* in choosing you as their partner in this journey. It also shows very clearly that you have the ability to guide the client, to lead them through the maze of training with a level of self-confidence that they will, in time, come to admire as your ability to teach without lecturing, to lead without forcing, to inspire without dictating.

Most importantly, your client will trust the feedback, support and validation from your partnership and it will affect how they deal with challenges and obstacles in other parts of their lives. They will start to feel every obstacle in their lives dissipate, that they are capable of achieving any goal for as long as they put in the right effort. In many ways, this goes beyond the program's original intention of helping someone reach a physical ideal, or to assist them in their journey of feeling supported and validated. By training with you, by investing in the partnership, the client starts to feel something even stronger and more worthwhile—they start to feel how much you believe in them.

It is, of course, important to recognize that there is the next session, the next obstacle, the next series of workouts that is part of the macrocycle. By acknowledging their efforts and their specific accomplishments, you have identified the strengths upon which you will build their next challenge. Now it is important to communicate to the client that their recent accomplishments set them up to overcome their next challenge. Before we proceed with this idea of challenging our client in their next workout, we must consider the alternative routes.

Let us say, for example, that this client completed their series of pull ups. However, out of the 30 or so pull ups that they completed, about 10 of them were not "perfect". One possible way of managing their next workout is to challenge them to do all 30 pull ups with perfect form. Another possible route is to increase the number of pull ups from 30 to 40. Another route is to add an incremental load to the exercise by using a weight belt, so that the exercise becomes more challenging. These are all viable, doable, and valid approaches to challenge a client.

You must keep in mind that if you are creating a challenge for your clients to give it their best in their next session (and frankly in every session), the challenge must present both a display of effort and level of proficiency. Every client that you train wants to participate in the training that you have devised for them. The key word is *participate*. Regardless of the level of challenge, regardless of how beneficial it is for the client, regardless of what your expertise dictates, your ability to challenge your client is measured primarily by their willingness and eagerness to follow your lead, and participate in the challenge you have set forth.

If exercise science dictates that you should not proceed with 40 pull ups, because the 30 pull ups they did complete were not done with perfect form, consider first if the client would be willing to do the *same* 30 pull ups with a lower margin for error. If the client does not seem too eager about this prospect, this is a key indicator of what motivates your client to perform. Regardless of what you think is effective, it is irrelevant if your client is not engaged in the process of completing the task. They may do it, but they will not look forward to the session. And they will not necessarily look forward to your next "challenge."

The primary purpose of creating a challenge for a client is to ensure two things: first, to make sure that they are progressing consistently, and second, to ensure that they are engaged in the process. It is important for the trainer to understand that, in some instances, these two things are *mutually exclusive*, and the trainer must be keenly aware of what motivates the client. If you follow the P.A.C.T. approach to managing your client's sense of engagement, more often than not, you will find that the challenge motivating them is the one that *leverages their strength* when they are faced with a task they did not imagine they could complete at all. In other words, you must know your client so well that you will create a challenge that both advances their progress and that they will be eager to complete. The best trainers and leaders know what motivates their people. There may have been a time when it was possible to motivate people by magnifying their constraints (i.e. "you did 30 pull ups, but 10 were shaky, so we need to do it again perfectly before we proceed"), but members and clients respond to trainers who leverage their strengths as a way of getting them to face challenges that they have never faced before.

As beneficial and challenging 30 perfect pull ups may seem, the client may see the task as unimaginative and uninspiring if it has been completed before with an acceptable degree of success. Clients invest in challenges that provoke their imagination, something that they never saw themselves doing. Tapping into the client's imagination requires an uncommon level of connectedness and leadership on the part of the trainer.

"THEN SHALL ALL OUR NAMES FAMILIAR"

Susan once remarked to me that if it were not for her kicking me out of the office, I would be working 7 days a week. So it was on a lazy Sunday afternoon that I was at the gym to get in a quick workout, shower, then hop into my office for a quick series of emails to prepare for the week. Usually, I ran a series of reports that track my division's progress, as well as individual progress. Often I would send out emails to individual trainers who had a good week, congratulating them on their achievement, and encouraging them to greater success.

That week, while reviewing my reports, I saw that Hal's report had reached a "Breakout" peak (I will explain further in the Business Development section of the book what the Breakout Model is, and its significance to a trainer's growth and progress). Almost two months after he and I had that talk in my office, he exceeded my original goal for him. He now had 13 active clients to his name, which meant that he was about to breakout and become a full-time trainer. This full-time status meant that not only had his hard work paid off, but that he would now join the ranks of senior trainers who make a consistent, full-time living at personal training. His passion, his warmth, his tirelessness, had all paid off. His hour had finally come, and he would receive his congratulatory email from his friend and manager. This email would punctuate a triumphant return to form for my previously beleaguered protégé.

I sent the email to Hal, which was full of praise and highlighting his accomplishments against the backdrop of his previous challenges. I was fully expecting to hear from him within the next hour. In fact, one of the things that made him very successful and likeable was his commitment to answering emails quickly—from clients, his colleagues, and especially his manager. By doing this he constantly made every one of us feel that he was always available, that he was always there. Susan was so impressed by Hal's quick-response to her emails that she would subsequently nickname him "Old Reliable."

As I finished up my emails and reports, I realized that I had been in the office a couple of hours. I put on my jacket, but before leaving I checked my phone for emails. There were a few from members who had questions about upcoming specials on training packages. A few more about upcoming group classes for the summer. As I was about to leave, I received an email from Hal. He said he needed to have a meeting with me, and that it was rather urgent. I agreed to meet him the following day.

The next day, Hal came to my office, accompanied by my two superiors. Susan and I were a little surprised, because we were not sure what the meeting was going to be about. The three of them had a seat in my little office. Everyone was all smiles, the mood was hearty, but not a word was spoken. Eventually I had the urge to speak.

"Everyone looks great, but what is this about?"

"We are taking Hal from you", said one of my superiors. "He has done such a great job with his clients, and we have heard such glowing things about him from his peers that we are actually here to ask your permission, and to get your thoughts."

"Where are you taking him? You can't do that! He's ours!" joked Susan.

My second superior replied "We are creating a very special role for him, but it will be a role that he is going to define. It is still very much in the beginning phases, but it will have a great emphasis on service, hospitality, and making sure that every member feels heard and appreciated."

"I'm not sure what to say. Of course we are happy for him," I replied. I was overjoyed for him, to see him so well appreciated, for his work to have been acknowledged.

"This is great to hear," my superior said. We would like to have him start next week, which means he will be leaving you soon."

"Oh, so you mean he will be offsite? Yes, yes of course, I didn't realize that by creating this role he would actually not be working here anymore..." At this point I understood that Hal's promotion would actually take him away to a completely different location, a different realm altogether. He was not only being promoted, he was on his way to creating his own mark, claiming his own crown.

"The project isn't quite ready yet, but once it is completed, it requires someone of Hal's talents. It will be for an elite client base, and his ability to communicate, his knowledge of personal training, his accomplishments, is absolutely without question. But yes, the project will take him to a very special place. We are delighted for him." My superiors had so much confidence in him that I nodded in acknowledgement and acquiescence. This was Hal's time.

"My liege," Hal looked at me. "Can I go? May I take my final leave of you?"

"Yes, Hal. You are the prince of this division. Our prince. This is who you are, and who you will always be."

As everyone stood, I instructed Susan to walk them to the front door. Once they left, I sat on my chair, then turned my head to look out of my office window, which gave me a clear view of the gym floor. This allowed me to see what was happening at all times. A member walked by. He looked at me, smiled and waved, before walking towards the cardio area. He was an older gentleman, one of Hal's best clients. He went to grab a towel and threw it over his shoulder before getting on a treadmill to start his warm-up by walking. All the treadmills in the cardio area were full and working. Some members were walking a calm and easy pace, like Hal's client. Some were jogging and sweating. Right next to them were the benches where members were lifting weights or checking their phones for emails. Some were training with members of my team—Hal's teammates. They were all smiling and joking, hi-fiving. They were happy. They were training.

As Hal was being walked up the stairs to create his future and his destiny, I realized that had I not told him to do this for himself, Hal would have been out there doing the same thing at around this time— handing out his towels, or hi-fiving the members who would later become his clients. He would have been flashing his smile, and making friends with everyone he met. I had seen him do this many times on this very floor. Had I not let him go, he would have been content to make this floor his happy, familiar kingdom. It was on this floor that he first shook my hand, and told me that he was game.

Looking out of that clear window, I realized that I would never see Hal on that floor again.

In the many months that followed, I heard stories of his many victories, that his new exclusive project was something special indeed. He was not only successful, he had become famous. He developed his own team, his own curriculum, and he taught them exactly what to do. One day he invited me to this special location, which at that point had reached mythical proportions.

"I know ye not, old man," he joked, as he greeted me at the door. I laughed at his joke. He had grown in poise and confidence.

I almost did not recognize him—he moved with such a calm confidence. He also seemed bigger, much stronger, incredibly fit. He showed me the beautiful space with new floors, new equipment. Yet the air in the room was different—it was cool to breathe, like I had entered a sanctuary. He introduced me to his team, and they were all very welcoming and happy to see me. He told me that he wanted the team to remain small, only to a select few. "A happy few," he said. When I asked him why, he replied "smaller teams are faster teams. Communication, execution, error rates are all better managed when the scope is kept to a manageable but expert few." He spoke like the Henry we both admired.

When I left and returned to my old division, I looked briefly at the floor, scanning it not only for what was going on right then, but also for what it once was. Sometimes, I still I imagine him on that floor, eager, knowledgeable, confident, an expert in what he was being paid to do. A young man whose dreaming found the place where his dreams could come true, where he could wear something similar to a crown, something he could wear full of pride. This is the image Hal left for me in my own mind and it is an image which I like to think is the face of the personal trainer: well trained, sure-footed in his expertise, a guy who can convince you he is good at what he does, someone who is not just there to watch you sweat, but an expert who knows what to do and can inspire you to "give it your best shot". In other words, someone who can make a difference in everyone's life.

THE PRICE OF LEADERSHIP

Leadership is perhaps the hardest skill to develop for many personal trainers, yet it is the most vital. Leadership encompasses many qualities, such as vision, compassion, connectedness, and decisiveness. Although there are many books that cover leadership from the perspective of its necessity and benefits, very few speak about the *experience* of leadership. More specifically, few really speak about the cost of leadership.

In many client-facing industries, there has been much discussion of the concept of likeability, the key quality that makes a potential client or customer warm-up to you. The purchasing experience is positively affected by a likeable persona, and the way you communicate with a potential client. It is an observable phenomenon and quite worthy of study. The likeability factor plays a key role in leadership.

The difficulty in utilizing likeability comes when the client objects to an idea that the trainer has proposed. In the relationship between you and your client, regardless of its length of time, there will always come a time when a client will offer an objection to a suggestion or a challenge, and you will simply have to manage it in order for both of you to arrive at a "win-win" scenario. The difficulty in implementing likeability occurs when likeability becomes confused with "being liked." Or more specifically, being liked all the time. For example, if you offer an exercise to a client, and the client objects to the selection, saying that it is too difficult, there is an opportunity for you to either progress or regress the selection, based on the client's feedback and explanation of why they don't want to participate. Or, if a client offers an objection to the fee structure of their sessions, you can offer alternatives, like a more affordable package of training sessions.

Tension also occurs when a trainer proposes an idea to a client thinking that the client will like them *more*. This is a natural inclination—as social human beings we want to have pleasurable and positive social interactions. When we propose an exercise or program or strategy or goal that does not endear us to our client, we will have reached a defining moment in the relationship that will affect its direction and tone. During such moments, it is important to keep two things in mind:

- The relationship between the two of you is based on your ability to lead the client to success through your technical expertise, and your belief in your client's ability to succeed.
- Your client has to constantly believe in—and be reminded of—the vision of the journey you have created together, and the satisfaction they will experience when they achieve the goals of the program.

Both your technical expertise and your belief in your client's ability to succeed determine the nature of the relationship. Your client, during such difficult moments, must be reminded of that fact, along with the inspiring vision of where they will arrive when they achieve the goals of the program.

At no point, however, should you ever consider a decision that will make you more likeable to the client. Your client does not have to like you—you need them to be committed to the relationship and its vision, because it can compromise the nature of the relationship and the vision of the program if they do not. Whether the client likes you or not, the basic integrity of your technical expertise, customer care, and leadership ability relies solely on whether you and the client commit to your ability to train them, believe in them, and guide them towards the vision of the program.

When you remind your client of this fundamental aspect of their training, especially during a conversation when they offer an objection, your client may very well agree with you, but may express a comment about *you* that may not be so palatable. While the comment may be undeserved, it is a common experience among trainers—we do the right thing for the client, and the client agrees to the idea, but they do not necessarily like you for it.

Compliance on the part of the client is achieved through effective management. Compliance, combined with understanding, is achieved through persuasiveness and education. This goal is reached when the client not only complies with your directions and understands the goal of the program, but they also believe that you care about them personally. That is a feat that is achieved by leadership. Likeability alone cannot achieve this; leadership is also necessary. Only a trainer who has accepted that honing their technical expertise and customer care skillsets will be able to convince a client of their commitment to their development and to the judiciousness of the vision that has been laid before them. This may seem like a beneficial component of being a leader, but there is a hidden cost.

That cost is isolation. A leader travels ahead, and travels alone. A leader seeks completion and success, not approval. The experience of leadership is in part defined by constant and often unnerving silence. You cannot afford to listen to anything that compromises your partnership, your vision of excellence, your professionalism, and your integrity. That silence, and the pressures that accompany it, combine to make leadership a somewhat uninviting experience, which is why it is reserved for the brave and the few.

To achieve a true partnership between client and trainer requires a level of compassion, maturity, and leadership that falls mostly on the shoulders of the trainer who quietly accepts it. That maturity can only be arrived at when it becomes clear that your investment in your client's success is a gift that your client can never return. This is the reality of customer care, leadership, and the profession that you have chosen: you have to be *tough* to do this. The toughest thing you will ever have to accept in personal training is that no matter what your client says to you that may feel negative or discouraging, your belief in their ability to succeed must never waver, and your commitment to their journey must never falter. This means that your customer care and leadership capabilities must be coupled with the ability to manage pressure at very extreme levels. The hourly rate that your client pays you covers the product and the service, but never think that your selflessness, kindness, and your toughness will ever be adequately compensated. Your client will never understand you the way you understand them. Your client can never care about your goals or share in your challenges or support you, the way you care about their goals and help them with their challenges, and support them every step of the way. When your client is having a bad day, it is you that they share this with. And more often than not, it is you that turns their mood around for the better, through intelligent exercise selections and the appropriate positive reinforcement. Your client, no matter how much they say they care about you, is not in a position to do the same for you should you have a bad day.

Leadership is effective and intelligent selflessness, to be connected to others yet resolutely firm. Anyone can talk back, hit back, or talk about someone behind their back. It takes toughness and uncommon grit to fulfill your mission, for the benefit of your client, and for the success of your business. It is a dedication to excellence for its own sake, a standard that you personally uphold. That standard will guide you and your client to your shared vision and the challenges that will put both of you to the test. When you both arrive at a challenge, more often than not the astuteness of the program will unravel the problem. However, when it is the client who offers the challenge through an objection, it is your ability to accept the realities of leadership that will resolve it.

THE THIRD COMPETENCY

SALES

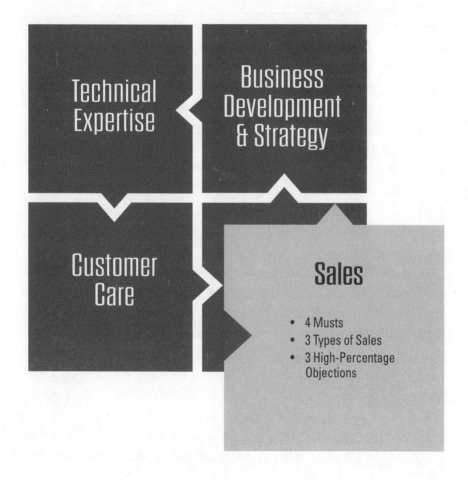

Technical Expertise

Business Development & Strategy

Customer Care

Sales
- 4 Musts
- 3 Types of Sales
- 3 High-Percentage Objections

I f you do not have clients to train—if no one is buying the product and services that you are selling—you have no business to manage. You cannot call yourself a professional trainer. You are a hobbyist at best, and you are certified out of love for a subject, as opposed to doing what is necessary to ensure that your business is profitable. Sales skills are a necessity for a trainer—you cannot train if you are not selling.

What makes trainers hesitant to approach sales with a sense of eagerness is the fact that most of us are product-oriented professionals. In the simplest terms, trainers devote the majority of their time and effort ensuring that their products are of the highest quality, and deliver the highest value. Trainers take great pride and comfort in their programs and their education because, at the end of the day, this technical expertise constitutes much of the product and service we provide. However, regardless of the quality of your product and expertise, your efforts will be for naught if no one knows they need it. In other words, no matter how good the product is, it is useless if no one needs it. It is important to approach the idea of sales less from the perspective of how good your product is, and focus your efforts toward identifying the needs of your intended market. If we as fitness professionals carefully identify the needs of our member base and potential client base, we can design our product and services so that it caters to those particular needs.

The sales process becomes easier if you can identify the individuals who need what you are offering. A pen cannot be sold to someone who does not think that he needs a pen, no matter how beautifully constructed the product is or how affordable the price. However, if that same person is about to sign a $50 million contract, and the only available writing instrument is the pen you have, she may just give you $10 million for the pen in order to get $40 million upside.

Sales is not about making someone need your product—it is the process of helping the individual identify *their* need, which gives you the opportunity to create the product that promises to fulfill that need, and delivering it with a unique service that ensures that what the client is receiving is of the highest quality. Most trainers confuse the sales process with the amount of money the client says they have and are willing to pay in exchange for your product and services. What adds to the confusion is that we tend to believe that if a client questions the price of our product, we put pressure on ourselves for either not creating a better product, and/or our ability to deliver value that is somehow subpar. Neither of these are completely true.

The process of sales has *nothing to do with money*. Sales is about fulfilling a need that the potential client has or has become aware of, while you supply the product and service that promise to fulfill that need. By focusing on identifying what the potential client needs, the trainer develops the ability to identify what products and services are already in their toolbox that can serve the client's needs best. The trainer should not invest their time and effort designing programs and paradigms solely based on previous experience and expertise, because this can limit not only their ability to identify the needs of their potential clients, they may also miss an opportunity for further education because they have not identified a completely untapped market. This approach to sales is far more marketing-focused than sales-focused; it is more about listening and observing closely what the member needs, as opposed to fashioning a quality product that no one wants.

KEEP LOOKING

Ideally, once you have identified a particular client's needs, and you have the expertise and customer care to deliver what they are looking for, the financial transaction should essentially go without a hitch. While this is a logical conclusion, the reality is often different. From experience I can tell you that potential clients will, more often than not, offer some sort of objection to your offering and to its pricing. Here the best strategy is to focus on what the client is looking for, as opposed to focusing your energies on constantly justifying the virtues of your product.

The question then becomes: what is the client truly looking for?

If the macrocycle creates a vision for the client, and our role as fitness leaders is to inspire our clients by leading them towards that vision, we can safely assume that what every member is looking for is to come closer to the vision of themselves that is inspiring, achievable, and fulfilling. What every member is looking for, once they join a gym, is to get closer to this vision of themselves. Someone capable, someone in control, someone who has the ability to set their mind to something and, by dint of hard work and honest effort, achieve their goals and reap the benefits.

Most clients will tell you what they think their goals are, but your job is to discern and understand what those goals mean to *them*, and what achieving them will bring to their lives. It is important for you to discover this for yourself because your client may not be able to verbalize to you, or even to themselves, what they are looking for. Let us more closely examine some common goals that trainers hear from potential clients, and what they could possibly represent:

- Lose 15 pounds
- Get more ripped
- Be more toned
- Increase strength
- Add more muscle mass
- Be more defined

On one level, one can infer that the client has these goals for somewhat vain reasons because they are associated primarily with their appearance. In the fitness field, these goals tend to be received with a slightly derisive attitude, because they are considered superficial and, to a certain extent, show the limited knowledge of a client with regards to athletic and functional performance.

We tend to be a little more receptive to goals that do not necessarily have an aesthetic bent, and more towards what we deem "functional".

- Increase deadlift by 50 pounds
- Increase bench press by 25 pounds
- Reduce marathon time by 40 minutes
- Improve sprint time by 2 seconds

These goals tend to be greeted with more eagerness by fitness professionals because they are more correlated towards athletic performance, which can then be correlated with some level of increased functionality in daily life. A strong deadlift and a strong bench press will somehow make an individual stronger for daily activities and life in general. These aesthetic goals and performance goals require certain types of programs and specific approaches. The important question is: what does achieving any of these goals *specifically mean to the client?*

If a client loses 15 pounds, increases their deadlift by 50 pounds, and increases their bench press by 25 pounds in one year, how do these achievements directly impact the life of that client? If we are addressing how it directly changes their life, chances are very little. Unless a client is in a profession (such as a professional athlete) where an increase in strength will improve performance, one can argue that increased functional strength has little impact. Even if they lose 15 pounds and get more ripped, these achievements will not necessarily directly impact their lives unless a client is in a profession in which they directly affect their ability to earn a living.

Most of our clients are trying to achieve these goals for less than functional and practical reasons. A client will never get a promotion in their job because they lost 15 pounds (unless they are in a profession where appearances play a major part in their job description). A client will never improve their ability to be a parent or friend by improving their physical capability.

There is a *deeper and more personal* reason why clients constantly request the same physical goals. If you understand the reasoning behind these requests, you will better manage the sales process.

THE TANK

I was going to make him wait a little bit. I was told that this potential candidate for my personal training team had a very confident manner to him. I was also told by another source that he had a lot of confidence, but could be helped in the manners department. He would need mentoring and guidance, in order for him to understand how the company I was hiring for works.

I was also told that he had interviewed at two other locations, and was turned down. The reason? *Over*-confidence. He had the education, the certifications, but he came on too strong, and these managers were concerned that their members would not take to his strong personality.

So I made him wait. Trainers need enough confidence to face the challenges and pressures of our profession, but too much confidence can lead to impatience. Impatience leads to the kind of reactivity that makes a trainer say the wrong things at the wrong time. After 15 minutes, I went upstairs to greet my candidate.

He was sitting in one of the lounge chairs that is often reserved for members. He had a hulking and intimidating frame, which he somehow managed to fit in a white button-down shirt. The oxford print tie did not hide his athleticism and sheer physical presence. He saw me and smiled. I didn't smile back. Instead I approached him steadily, deliberately. I looked him in the eyes, to see if he would blink or show any wavering. It was a trick I had used in many of my interviews.

His physique was more suited for workout gear, as opposed to a suit and tie. But his eyes did not waver—they were steely, eager, and determined. He had the eye of the tiger.

I shook his hand as he stood up. He towered over me by a full foot. In my head I had already nicknamed him: The Tank. I said to him:

"You're hired. Follow me."

THEIR VISION

Each client comes to the gym with a story of how they see themselves and how they would like to see themselves. A client looking to transform their physiques, whether on an aesthetic level or on a performance level, is trying to achieve a vision of themselves that they feel is incomplete without having achieved these goals. Whether they are trying to lose 100 pounds or 10 pounds, trying to bench press 200 pounds or 50 pounds, the achievement of these goals represents a need to change how they currently perceive themselves. The client is going to come to you with a series of relative data that pertains to how they currently see themselves, and where they would like to go. Much of this data will involve their history, the sports they played, their previous fitness level, their injury history, and their surgery history, among other things. It will also involve how they feel about their current fitness level, what they would like to achieve during their time in the gym, and how it would all feel once they achieve their goals. You can refer back to the chapter on technical expertise for a full discussion on how we reconcile relative data with relevant data to paint a full illustration of where the client can go while training with you.

However, when it comes to sales—when it comes to truly understanding the individual member—it is important to go further in order to understand what the member is looking for at the deepest level. At this stage in your partnership, the potential client may very well be completely convinced that you are able to help them achieve their goals. What is very important, at this stage, is your ability to identify *why* they need to achieve these goals, why they need to train, and what all of it means to *them*. Once you can identify this, you have identified what they are looking for—and this is your opportunity to position and adapt your product to suit their particular needs.

This approach to sales gives you a more proactive position when meeting with a potential client. You are now actively listening and searching for clues so you can understand the individual sitting across from you. This potential client is not just a number, not just another member—this is a person whose fascinating story will help you overcome your own anxieties about your ability to train them, to sell them a package of sessions, and hopefully become a successful trainer. This person's story, if you listen closely, will help you understand that every member is in fact looking for the same thing: a way to inspire themselves, a way to transform themselves into something better. They want to partner with someone with a similar vision, someone whose expertise will not only guide the partnership, but whose leadership will help them through the challenges and setbacks that reaching any goal must entail.

THE 4 MUSTS

- Assume You Will Close the Sale
- Establish Your Expertise
- Ask, Then Listen
- Small Yes, Big Yes

1) ASSUME YOU WILL CLOSE THE SALE

Your potential client has agreed to meet with you for their initial assessment. Keep in mind that this prospect has made several decisions by agreeing to meet with you:

- They consider the meeting important because they have allocated their first resource into the process of becoming your client—they have invested their time.
- By investing time, they are open to the possibility of trusting that the process will be beneficial for both parties.
- There is already a substantial level of investment on the part of the potential client even before you have started the in-take process.
- They have already started to think about how they want to go about achieving their goals.

Assuming that you will close the sale allows you to enter that appointment with confidence, and view the meeting as a platform on which your technical expertise can be showcased. More importantly, you can enter into the appointment knowing that the investment process, on the part of the client, has already begun, even before they have had the chance to see what is truly in store for them. In this position, you must keep one thing in mind—the client has already started the investment process.

2) ESTABLISH YOUR EXPERTISE

Once you meet your client, it is important to establish early on that they have made a good decision by meeting with you. One way to assure the client that this is the case is by establishing your knowledge of your chosen field, that you are educated, and that you are capable of backing the product that they are looking to purchase.

When your prospective client refers to their shoulder, refer to the shoulder via their anatomical terminology (i.e. the glenohumeral joint, scapulo-humeral rhythm, insertion points of the long head of the triceps, latissimus dorsi and teres major, etc.). The client need not understand the exact meaning of the terminology. They don't need that clarification (the purpose of educating a client is, ultimately, to reassure them that their investment in you is a smart decision)—what they do need is reassurance that you are an expert in the field, that you are capable of managing their fitness portfolio, and that you can do so on a level that is unmatched by others.

3) ASK, THEN LISTEN

In these meetings, the person who is constantly asking questions is the one in charge of the meeting. The client has expressed their need to change, and you, as the trainer, must supply the reassurance that you have the tools and capability to augment that change.

This position of control, for the trainer, is greatly magnified by this simple realization: the client believes that they are in control. This is advantageous because this allows your client to feel relaxed. It is your job, during these question and answer sessions, to ensure that the following are accomplished:

a) By believing they are in *control*, they are more willing to divulge important data—*relative* data.

b) By asking questions, you are giving them the impression that they have a *choice*.

You have started to change their lives, and they have not even purchased their package of sessions with you.

4) SMALL YES, BIG YES

Start the process of being agreeable early, and as frequently as possible. This concept of "small yes, big yes" is relatively easy to implement. Essentially, we ask questions that the client can easily agree to. By doing so, you are accruing a series of agreements that leads to your "big yes"—do they want to start training with you by purchasing a package of training sessions?

As much as you want the client to say yes to you, you have to also find things that you can say yes to. This "win-win" approach creates a dynamic and reciprocal interaction that keeps you proactive and positive in the communication.

These "4 Musts" of sales lay the groundwork for every interaction that you have with your client. Think of how powerful your positive influence would be on every individual that you interact with simply by assuming that you can supply them with what they are looking for, that you are establishing your competence, that you are endlessly curious about them, and somehow manage to be agreeable throughout the entire interaction. More importantly, imagine how positive your influence would spread once you have a stable base of clients, and every interaction that you had with them came from a foundation of intelligent and highly aware communication? If you can imagine this, you can start to picture the significance of your role as a personal trainer, beyond someone who counts reps and spots a client during a lift.

FUZZY MATH

October is a surprisingly busy season for training. Many clients return from summer vacation, with a sense of renewed purpose.

Perhaps it is because many have not been faithful to their training programs and nutrition plans, so October becomes a second opportunity to achieve their year's goals. What is, however, more relevant to you, is the fact that the 4th quarter of the fiscal year is also another opportunity to finish the year strongly from the perspective of work-performance. These two aspects of a member's life converge in October.

In the middle of October, the Tank entered my office to see where he stood in the rankings of numbers of clients. He had been on the team for 4 months and wanted to prove his worth; on the floor he was simply on fire. The Tank, I found out during his interview, had been rejected by several other clubs, and he seemed to be using this opportunity with my team as a type of vengeance ride. He wanted to prove his worth. He knew that to be the best, he needed the numbers to show for it. He accrued an impressive number of clients—25. It seemed like every member he spoke to instantly became his friend and client. I sometimes felt that they didn't have much choice, considering how persuasive, determined, and forceful he could be. The Tank had done well for himself in the few months since I hired him. He was unstoppable on many levels. My team had never seen anyone like him before—affable but intense. His clients were getting results, but they were also a little intimidated by him.

He had taken to a little practice I gave him when he first started: write down your goals on a piece of paper, and review them once or twice daily so that the goals became an intrinsic part of his being. The Tank, however, modified the practice by taking a copy of my final report from last month, which showed the current rankings of each trainer in the club and obsessed over that, instead of his goals. The Tank was driven to say the least.

The Tank tapped me on the shoulder while I was working on October's reports. Before I could turn, he grabbed my shoulder, and looked at the report I was working on. He studied the screen closely.

"Where am I there?" He asked me.

"Tank, you're number three."

"Yeah, I can see that. Why am I number three?"

"You don't have enough clients yet. You need just two more clients to beat Brian." Brian has been our number one producer going on 3 years now, so I didn't see the problem with Tank being number three, especially since he had only been there a few months.

"But I have 3 new clients. I converted them two days ago."

"Tank," I explained, "if they have not actually purchased, they cannot go on this report. When they purchase, you will be number one. Sound good?"

Suddenly, The Tank let go of my shoulder, stood up straight and started to walk out of the office. He opened the door, and said, "Your math is wrong! I'M number ONE!"

"No Tank", I tried to explain, "you will be number one, you just need..."

"No no no, that's fuzzy math you're doing there, your math is wrong. I'M number ONE!"

The door slammed, and my office is silent again. Susan looks at me, and she starts laughing. "You hired him. Eye of The Tiger cannot be stopped!" Then the door opened again, and it was The Tank.

"Yes Tank...", I meekly tried to get out.

"I'M NUMBER ONE!!!" The door slammed shut again. Through the office window Susan and I could see him huffing and puffing, agitated and on the prowl. His teammates knew that look. It meant that The Tank was on the hunt for a new client to his roster.

Now he was on the floor, doing what made him the best. 30 minutes later, he was back. "I got 3 people on the floor to buy packages from me. They went upstairs to purchase. They should be in your system now."

"Tank, how did you..."

Before I could finish my question, The Tank asked, "Now am I number one?"

I didn't have to look at the report. "Yes Tank."

The Tank smiled winningly. "I told you I was number one."

THE 3 OBJECTIONS

An objection from the client to the product and service being offered must be handled primarily as a form of inquiry. When a potential client offers an objection, at first it may be difficult to not take them at face value. If you remember to assume that you've already made the sale, it will help you clarify your purpose. They are there to get in shape; they understand they cannot do it on their own; they want to confirm that spending time with you will be both productive and enjoyable, which will require a substantial amount of investment on their part. Your purpose is to constantly illustrate, through the clear communication of relevant and relative data, how they will benefit from training with you.

When an objection is offered, you will be tempted to defend the quality of your product. You will be tempted to justify your knowledge, your expertise, your experience, your purpose. You have to be tougher than that. You have to remember that your client is there to change, they are there to achieve their goals, and you can handle these objections more expertly if you use this opportunity to remind them of that. The client will see how you manage objections in general, which then gives them a preview of what it will be like to work with you.

There are 3 common objections from a client when it comes to investing in personal training sessions:

- Price
- Scheduling
- Autonomy

Before we go through the client's rationale behind each objection, keep in mind that a potential client is seriously considering purchasing sessions because they desire to reach a particular level of fitness, and have not succeeded in achieving that level on their own, or with another trainer. In other words, by not reaching that goal before, there is little chance that they can reach it without you.

The most common objection that people offer is about price. It is the one that is offered in practically all industries, because there is a desire for a discount on the product and service. Though the request for a lower fee occurs in other industries, trainers are particularly susceptible to this objection because they desire to help clients, and feel that they are helping them by giving them a break on their fees. If they cannot afford your services, then they should seek the services of another trainer; you are not the individual to help them with their finances. In reality, a client's objection to the price is a general practice of inquiry into what you are offering. It is not a cue for you to start discounting what you are offering.

Scheduling sessions is another objection clients will offer, and a trainer may view this as a cue that the potential client may not be as committed to training as they had previously perceived. If the scheduling objection is raised alone, it is generally a good sign: they have not objected to the price of your services. This allows room for you to display a good level of active listening skills, because the potential client is giving you more information about their lives as a whole.

The final common objection is the autonomy objection: the client can work out on their own. We can generally presume that the client has the *capability* to do so, but it is highly unlikely that they can achieve the results on their own that they can by working with you. By keeping this in mind, you can clearly communicate to the client why they have come to you to begin with – they want results that they cannot achieve on their own, and they need us to get there.

The most important consideration in handling any objection is that it sets the tone for the relationship, even before the first training session begins. You will not just be training this client to help them achieve results, but you will be doing so as a professional who deserves to be respected for your passion, dedication, and expertise. Managing a client's objections requires that you communicate proficiency and confidence in your skills. You, the fitness professional, are capable of listening to their concerns, but you are also capable of making it very clear that you are an expert at what you are doing, and that they need you in order to achieve their optimal result. Establish this tone now, and your relationship with this client will be based on mutual respect and benefit.

THE 3 TYPES OF SALES

In the previous section I showed you how sell your product and services to a client who needs them, but also to establish the appropriate tone for the trainer/client relationship. How you utilize each sales approach below can be based as much on the situation as it is on how you view your product, your service, and your overall level of proficiency. However, keep in mind that regardless of which approach you choose to implement, be mindful that it will establish the tone of the relationship.

Negotiating: This sales approach is a type of concession to the client's objections, where there is a desire on the part of the trainer to validate these objections by negotiating a set of terms that are a compromise between what the trainer proposes and what the client wants to pay.

Keep in mind that what we are looking for is complete success for both the client and the trainer; the "win-win" that benefits both parties. In these types of scenarios, concession or compromise is not part of the discussion. Generally, when a compromise is reached, the outcome is that it is the *trainer* who ends up compromising and being on the losing end.

The negotiating approach, which is founded on compromise, approaches each objection with compromise as its essential theme. Here are some examples:

- A trainer's hourly rate for sessions is $150 an hour, and that a package of 10 sessions is $1,500. The client balks at the fee, and says that it is far too expensive and outside of their budget. The negotiating approach offers a simple solution: purchase 10 sessions, and the trainer will offer two sessions "on the house."
- A trainer offers one-hour sessions, but the client says that they can only do half-hour sessions. The trainer offers to honor the client's request, and trains them only for half-hour slots, and only charging them the full-hour rate when two 1-hour sessions have been *completed*.
- The trainer offers a structured program that can lead the client to success, but the client does not want a program or their assistance. Instead, they propose that the trainer write them a program that they can follow. The trainer obliges the request by writing them a program, and offers to train them twice a month, to see how they are progressing.

In each scenario it is the trainer who compromises on each objection. Although the trainer has closed the sale and added to their roster, they have achieved it at a significant cost.

In the first case, a precedent has been set, and now the client will come to expect that the relationship will proceed based on what has been agreed upon, regardless of whether or not they achieve the results they are looking for.

If we examine how a negotiating approach handles the pricing objection, the client will now come to expect two sessions *every time they renew their package*. By establishing the precedence that you are willing to concede on price, they will come to expect this particular benefit—simply because this is what has been established from the beginning. They will continue to expect it for as long as they are training with you, because they see no valid reason to not give it to them every time.

The same goes for the scheduling objection—once half-hour routines are established. If half-hour sessions were viable, they should continue to be viable, in order for the agreement to continue—at least from the perspective of the client.

It should be clear that the negotiating approach puts you in a position of constantly conceding to the client's wishes, which erodes the respect and confidence you were seeking to establish in the relationship. This should be of grave concern to you for a very simple reason: the client has essentially trained you. You are not a fitness professional in the eyes of this client, you are now a simply a salesperson who needs to move inventory. This is a not a desirable position.

That said, it is important to view the negotiating approach from the perspective of customer service. While this approach can potentially erode your professional credibility in the eyes of a client, in situations where the objection is based on a customer care issue, implementing the negotiating approach is very effective. For example:

The prospective client is ready and eager to train with you, but they offer the scheduling objection because they have family obligations that allow them to be at the gym only for a limited amount of time. They are eager to train, but their current situation only allots them this limited amount.

In this situation, it is appropriate and effective to utilize the negotiation approach because the client will not view the approach as a concession, but rather as a sign of your flexibility and understanding. You are doing them a favor, and the relationship starts on the right note because you are exercising a level of customer care that does not compromise your service or the relationship. In fact, this approach under these circumstances greatly helps the relationship by having it start off on the right foot.

Consultative Sales: The consultative approach presumes that if the client is more *educated* about what it is we are offering, they will essentially make the commitment to train with us. Regardless of the objection, when you defend your offering you presume that if you educate your clients, they will clearly see the virtues and benefits of the product and service that they are being offered, and that the value in what trainers do, how they do it, and how the product that is offered is worth the client's investment because of the quality of the work, and the level of care that the trainer invested in it. The approach, in and of itself, can work on certain occasions, but it is unreliable in the field. The problem is that this approach is based on two premises that presumes the client is taking into account:

- Level of expertise put into the making of the product
- Level of education of the client about the product

The premise is flawed, from the beginning, because we are presuming that our clients need to be educated in our craft in order to make a decision, as opposed to building a relationship that comes from understanding the prospective client's concerns. The essential problem of the consultative approach is that it presumes that the prospective client, by virtue of being uneducated in the field of exercise science, *is making an uneducated choice* by not committing to training with us. This is problematic because if we are looking to build a relationship, we must be able to show that we are a partner in their journey, as opposed to being an educator who could potentially judge them if they make a decision in error.

This particular approach is the primary default we utilize when an objection is offered to us by our prospective client—we make an attempt to *educate* the client in the value of our services by talking to them about the product. As discussed previously, it is important that we keep the focus of these conversations on the need of the client to train and get fit by using both the relevant and relative data that we have collected. Do not let the conversation become a lecture about how beneficial it is to work out with a trainer, as opposed to reminding the prospective client why they came to you in the first place. The reason trainers do this is because they are, as trainers, primarily invested in technical expertise, which is the foundation of their product and offering. When they believe that their expertise is, in any way, deemed less than valued, they fall into the trap of being on the defensive.

For example:

- The prospective client offers the price objection, saying that the 10 pack of sessions is too expensive and out of their budget. The consultative approach would dictate that the trainer begins by speaking about the benefits of consistent training, the effects of good cardiovascular health, and how increased lean body mass helps with posture and balance. The trainer can also start talking about how their existing clients received similar benefits, how they have made the commitment and are seeing the subsequent results.

- The prospective client offers a scheduling objection, saying that training consistently 2-3 times a week is something that they cannot commit to regularly, because their current schedule is unpredictable. The consultative approach to this objection would speak to the benefits of regular training, and how lack of consistency will not reap the particular results that the prospective client is looking for. The trainer at this point can also speak to the necessity of consistency, and that it will ultimately benefit the client in the long term because the initial sacrifice and inconvenience is generally worth it

- The prospective client feels confident in their ability to workout on their own, and insists on working out solo, until they are ready to commit to something as regimented as a customized training program. The trainer using the consultative approach can educate the client about macrocycles, peaks, manipulating volume and intensity, and back-off cycles, explaining how they can create the appropriate environment for the prospective client's body to be challenged, adapt, and improve—none of which the client can achieve should they decide to work out on their own.

There is another fatal drawback to trying to educate the client in the value of what we do as a negotiating strategy—you will expend a substantial amount of energy *talking* about what you do when your energies should actually be focused on letting the prospective client do most of the talking. There are many reasons why active listening should be the primary skill you utilize in most of your interactions with members and clients, but the best reason is that you are *letting the client do all the work for you,* while we sit back and let them process the objection for themselves. When using the consultative approach, this scenario is reversed: we are the ones doing all the work and once again, the client is training the trainer to concede whenever an objection is offered. They have put the trainer in the position of having to constantly defend and justify their offering *before* committing to anything the trainer recommends—even if they already know that it is for their own benefit. This is a by-product of the consultative sales approach.

To further complicate matters (to the detriment of the trainer), all the client needs to do in order to justify the validity of their objections is to offer evidence why they are not completely convinced. If your goal is to educate your client on the benefits of personal training, *the burden of proof is on you to convince them that your product is 100% effective.* The prospective client does not have that same burden—they only need to prove that you are *slightly* ineffective to justify why they are not convinced. For example, you can list 10 major studies that prove that consistent and closely-monitored workouts that consist of weight training and cardiovascular training help reduce body fat, but all the prospective client has to do is mention anecdotal evidence of a friend who achieved similar results on their own in order to remain unconvinced that they should work with you. Your list of 10 major studies that you probably compiled over the course of several days is neutralized by a single unsubstantiated instance that proves that your offering is not effective 100% of the time. You may be 100% correct in your argument, but productive relationships do not start with someone being right and someone being wrong. All productive relationships start with two individuals who believe in the other person's ability to help the other. In this instance, whether the prospective client purchases sessions with you at this point is irrelevant—the relationship is now off on the wrong foot.

This situation can be very unpleasant, but it became unpleasant because the premise of the approach put you in an unpleasant situation—defending the value of your offering and the very significance of your profession. Learn to identify that, in such situations, falling into either approaches could potentially lead to instances where the prospective client is "training the trainer". Always remember that the prospective client is looking to start a very difficult journey of transformation, a journey they may have never started before. They are looking for someone to go on the journey with them, not someone to lecture them. When we partner in this journey with our clients, we ourselves start on our own journey of how to educate our clients by creating experiences that they can learn from, as opposed to teaching them about those experiences.

PARTNERSHIP SALES

The partnership sales approach is built upon the idea that you essentially understand where the client's objections are coming from. You can say this with confidence only if you put the assessment process in a priority category above the training program. The assessment has given you the opportunity to take in the client, categorize their data and manage it for them, so that your presentation is clear, illustrative, and convincing. This is a significant shift from the consultative approach, which relied heavily on designing an effective product based on your expertise. The partnership approach relies on a sophisticated data management protocol that is based on customer care, so that the end-presentation to the client is not about the program you have designed, but about how closely you have observed where they currently are in relation to where they want to go. In this way, the assessment process is closely related to the partnership approach—we are establishing a relationship with the prospective client that is based on what we have directly observed from their words and actions, and communicating to the client that we are reliable professionals that are worthy of their investment. We are worthy not just because we are experts in our chosen field, but because we care enough to manage them as unique individuals, and are fully invested in their journey of growth and achievement.

As a result, any objection offered by the prospective client will be managed for their benefit.

• The prospective client offers the price objection, saying that the package is very expensive. Using the partnership approach you say that you are *glad* that they mentioned the pricing structure, because it can start the discussion about how to proceed, and how the process of training with you would start. You can certainly mention that you understand that the package may be expensive, but it is your opportunity to *partner* these statements with your concern for their health in the form of your assessment of their fitness needs. In other words, agree with them that it is expensive, and that the process of training requires a significant investment, especially since their assessment has shown that they actually need the training. Perhaps they do not need to invest 10 sessions, but rather with 5 sessions, and you will manage it according to *their* experience along with your recommendations.

• The prospective client offers the scheduling objection, saying that work often demands that they are travelling every other week. This is another opportunity for you to state that you are glad that they mentioned scheduling, because it allows both of you the opportunity to start discussing the process of training, and how you can both work around a very busy and hectic schedule.

• If they offer that they can train on their own, and feel confident that they can achieve results on their own you can say that you are *glad* that they mentioned getting started on their training, because now the two of you can discuss how their progress can be tracked, and how you can be of use in monitoring their progress.

The partnership approach is very different from the previous two approaches in one significant respect: in the above conversations, you have removed the impact of the objection by treating it as another form of *data* that you can use to further position yourself as a partner in the client's fitness journey. In the negotiating and consultative approaches, you have essentially put yourself in *opposition* to the client and their objections. Why? Because of a flawed mindset that is prevalent among most personal trainers: if the assessment and complimentary sessions were implemented on an expert level, and the client has clearly expressed the need to train, there should be *no objections*. This mindset is based on an innate need many of us have to be right, and thinking that by being right, we have done the best thing for our clients. However, if this does not help us connect with our prospective clients; if it does not bring us to the awareness that we must also care for our clients, then our expertise will always make us resistant to hearing our client's feedback, because feedback represents that we may be wrong.

The partnership sales approach puts you in the mindset that managing the client's objection(s) is part of *your* own growth and development. It empowers you to be able to listen so intently to the client's needs that you are capable of making the decisions that will benefit both of you, while remaining calm, collected, and clear-headed. Most trainers will have a challenging time with this approach, because of their belief that their level of investment in their expertise gives them the rightful authority to make decisions independent of the client's objections or concerns. The partnership approach requires a great deal of maturity on your part because your confidence in your expertise and judgment cannot by shaken by a simple price or scheduling objection. Having the ability to listen to feedback, and not let it shake your confidence in your abilities is the mark of a true professional. Having this skill will take you far in a profession where it is important to be the perennial eye of the storm.

THE SCORE

I make it my ritual in the morning to greet my members first thing when I get in. It is Monday morning and the lively conversations often occur in between reps or while a member is running on the treadmill. They are animated discussing their weekend activities, and how getting back to the gym helps them dial back into reality. Nothing starts the week better than an invigorating workout in the morning, they tell me.

My real goal is to greet my team of trainers. Even if they are in the middle of a session, I make it a point to go up to them and shake their hand. They are important to me, and I make sure that they feel that. More importantly, I want their clients to see that. I want their clients to see that I am there to support them in their goals, but most importantly I am there to support their trainer. I shake hands with one of my top producers, who is training a new client. I smile and tell him he is doing a great job. As I walk away I hear the client say, "Who is the guy in the suit?" My trainer answers him, "He's my boss." Later my trainer would tell me that his client told him, "You must be really important if he took the time to shake your hand!"

That morning, I was looking for The Tank. After making my rounds, I saw him on the trainer's bench, which is next to my office.

"Tank, I know your best friend was proud of you."

"I know. What's the score?"

"What score Tank?"

"The score for the trainers. I know I have been out a week, but I just want to know where I stand."

"Tank, you're at number 5 for the club."

"Ok." He then stood up and walked slowly towards the machines. A couple of his friends walked to him, started talking to him. He seemed tired, even though he made an effort to converse. The Tank seemed to struggle just standing there.

I should have asked about the funeral. His best friend had passed away, after a long illness. He was basically like a big brother to Tank.

Later that day he came into my office. The Tank sat heavily in the chair. He seemed to want to talk, but nothing came out of him. I turned around to look at him, and in his eyes I saw the words he wanted to say, that he needed someone to help him say. That's when Susan turned around to talk to him.

"Tank, you're number 5. Even though you have been out a week."

"Yeah..."

"Are you done with your sessions, Tank", Susan asked. She moved her chair towards him, and leaned in his direction. "Have you eaten? You look like you've lost weight. We may have to give you a new nickname if you keep losing weight. What if you're not Tank-size anymore?" She wanted him to smile, but he just didn't have the strength.

"I'm not hungry." He then looked up at Susan, then asked her, "Can I just sit here please?"

She nodded and smiled, "Sure you can Tank. That's your chair now." Susan looked at me as if to say that she wanted me to let her do the talking to Tank. She then turned to him.

"Tank, a few months ago when I visited my sister, my little nephew would tell me he wasn't hungry. I would tease him and say I would eat up all the chocolates if he didn't eat. He said he didn't care. This went on for a day or so. Then in the middle of the night he came to my bed and said he wasn't feeing well. I turned on the lights, and I asked him what was wrong. I put my hand on his forehead and he had developed a very high fever. Turned out he had the flu. So for the next few weeks, I would get up in the middle of the night at 2AM because he would be crying. His fever would be so high, so he would throw his blanket to the floor."

"Yeah, I used to do that when I had the flu," Tank chuckled. "Even in college I was doing that. Used to piss off my best friend when..." he said, his voice trailing into a whisper. I almost saw him smile. I wanted to smile with him, but this wasn't my conversation to manage—it was Susan's.

"I don't think your best friend was angry, Tank, not at all," Susan consoled him. "He just loves you so much he would get frustrated at the sight of you being sick. The last thing on his mind was for you to be sick. I know my sister and I felt very helpless when I saw my nephew throw his blanket. He would throw up on himself, and we would clean him up, and there was nothing we could do...but tell him it would be ok."

The Tank nodded. His eyes started to well with tears. He was now in a different place, a different time.

"Tank, that was when I decided to accept the offer to apply for management. I didn't want to feel helpless when it came to my sister and nephew. I wanted to give them everything, and if I am going to do that for them, it would be worth it, no matter how difficult. The score didn't matter to me."

Susan then took Tank's hand, and held it tight and warmly.

"Tank, I know the score means everything to you. But I think I'm pretty sure that it didn't matter to your best friend. What mattered to him was you."

Tank then looked up at Susan, his eyes now full of tears. Susan, still holding Tank's hand, also started tearing up. She assured him very gently that it was ok that he threw the blanket on the floor. The Tank struggled for a moment to find the words, even though he didn't really need them. Finally, when he opened his mouth, just a few words came out of him.

"He...was holding my hand when he passed..."

MANAGING FLUCTUATIONS

The world of the personal trainer, by and large, exists in a controlled environment. The training session more often than not occurs within the safe walls of an indoor gym. Even an outdoor site for a workout is selected by the fitness pro and agreed upon by the client. The careful crafting of the training program ensures that the workout follows a planned sequence that needs to be strictly followed. Randomness does not necessarily factor into the reality of the trainer and the environment we are looking to create, for the simple reason that, if we are to measure progress accurately and comparatively, consistency must be implemented on every level.

However, the unpredictable nature of life creates opportunities that we need to capitalize on, or challenges that blindside us and test our creativity, adaptability, and instincts. Perhaps a treadmill we were hoping to use with our client is in use with another member. There are several simple choices that can overcome this unforeseen occurrence. Situations like this are speed bumps that can affect a routine, but there are also events that can affect the nature of our business success, which can at times threaten to push it to its limits. These types of challenges need to be overcome, in order for us to continue on our mission.

During the sales process you are not necessarily in a controlled environment, because the conversation is led by your potential client's concerns. It is often a personal trainer's first real taste of the uncertainty that can potentially affect their sense of professional identity and business integrity. The 3 common objections basically challenge our offering to our client—an offering that they expressed a need for. Managing this first setback, and learning to thrive during the process, will prepare you for the complicated but fascinating mechanisms that drive your overall business. The systems in place for a successful business prepare it for the constantly fluctuating nature of a business cycle. By studying and mastering the systems that support your passion for fitness, you will not only learn to manage the up and down cycle of any business, you will learn to thrive in them.

THE FOURTH COMPETENCY

BUSINESS DEVELOPMENT AND STRATEGY

Business Development and Strategy

- Core Values/Vision/Mission/ Strategic Objectives/Planning/ Tactical Switches/Targets
- 4 Business Models
- 3 Strengths
- Intensity and Persistence Principles

Technical Expertise

Customer Care

Sales

There is admittedly something admirable in training a client towards success without a single thought given to your own financial gain. It comes from an acute sense of selflessness, of wanting to give back, of simply enjoying the reward of seeing someone overcome a struggle and improve from the experience. Perhaps you feel that you should not need much in the material realm—that the only reality is that one gives selflessly for the benefit of others. However, the desire to see success in others is not sustainable if you do not apply the same vision of success to your own life. Before you proceed with this most important chapter, you must accept that the successful management of your business is determined by how carefully you implement a series of competencies. This final skillset, this final piece of the puzzle, is the most important.

The business development and leadership system taught in the 4C Method will help you become profitable and financially independent as a fitness professional. However, let us be clear that although financial independence will enable you to acquire material benefits, this is not your primary goal. Your goal is the development of a solid, resilient, and sustainable business, so that your primary mission of sharing your success with your clients remains similarly sustainable and prosperous.

BUILDING YOUR BUSINESS

You have heard the phrase "build your business", and have received the common prescriptions about increasing market presence, building brand equity, raising your rates, being selective with your core clients, and managing your time effectively. Though very sound advice if applied intelligently to specific markets and models, these prescriptions are not effective *starting points*. They do not tell you where to start, let alone how to start.

Building your personal training business starts with identifying the core values that you intend to represent in the work that you intend to share with your clients. This is a simple but necessary exercise, because you want your clients to be aware that the fitness regimen that you have customized for them is not just another run-of-the-mill/off-the-shelf product. You want your clients to understand that what they are receiving from you took thousands of hours of dedication. You want them to appreciate that you are driven by a passion for excellence and superior performance, and are addressing the individual needs and aspirations of each client that you have the privilege of training. You want your clients to see that they are receiving the very best of who you are as a professional.

You can only build if you know where to start. It starts with what you believe in. Clearly identifying where you should start your efforts in building your business will give you a sense of how you should proceed. Start, first and foremost, by identifying your core values. Identifying your core values starts the process of creating your professional identity, defining your offering, and sharing your passion with your intended market. More importantly, your core values guide you in the process of taking that professional identity in order to expand into your product, your processes, your brand, and your business. What you ultimately offer your clients is a physical representation of your innate quality as a cultivated individual and dedicated professional. This is exactly why you are not a "salesperson", because your level of investment is higher than your need to sell a product. You are more focused on sharing your beliefs and values with your intended market on a one-on-one level through fitness and exercise.

A sample list of core values:

- We believe in having PASSION for everything that we do.
- QUALITY above all else.
- Developing INDIVIDUALITY is our measure of effectiveness.
- PERFORMANCE is paramount.
- EQUALITY allows for a working environment that is inclusive, caring, and professional.

This brief sampling of core values (Passion, Quality, Individuality, Performance, and Equality) affords you two important opportunities. One, it allows you to clearly identify what is important to you as an individual, thereby helping you create your professional identity. If you identify with passion, quality, individuality, performance, and equality, you will implement these qualities in your professional tasks and duties, which then translate directly into your offering. You will also use them as personalized standards that you will not go below; standards that you are committed to reaching on a daily basis. You would not be who you are without these standards. By doing this, your work takes on a life of its own—associated with powerful adjectives that are immediately identified with excellence and being the best.

There is another advantage to creating a list of core values—it allows you the opportunity to share these values with your potential clients. You inspire a similar flame of passion for the product and service you offer when they are imbued with qualities that your clients share with you. Doesn't everyone believe in being passionate, in quality, in individuality, performance, and equality? A professional and a brand that represents these values will attract clients and customers who *share* those values. Your work is a reflection of your values as a professional and the brand that you represent, and when your clients choose you to partner with them in their journey, it is because they see in you the same core values and standards that they live by and uphold. Professionals who hold themselves to a high standard prefer to work with professionals who share similar standards.

RYAN

Tank told me that she was from Florida, and that her name was Ryan. Susan reviewed her resume with me, and she felt her qualifications were sound, and that she could grow with us. Tank, on the other hand, expressed concerns that she seemed to lack confidence during the phone interview, but they were confident in their ability to create superstars for our division.

When they brought Ryan into the office to start the interview, I saw someone full of positive energy. She was smiling and radiant, with a great handshake and overall great attitude. I asked her if she wanted to sit down, and she said that she would love to, but she asked if she could sit on a Swiss-ball instead. Tank went to the gym floor to get her one.

"Thanks Tank!" she said, smiling. She was winning me over, and I hadn't even asked her a question.

"Ryan, what brings you to personal training?"

. She talked about how she had been athletic all her life and had always loved fitness. " I just love how training makes me feel, how it relieves my own stress, and how it just makes me more positive throughout the day. It's just such a huge part of my life!"

Tank and Susan were smiling at this point. Everyone seemed to be in absolute agreement that what we had in front of us was a star in the making.

"What brought you into the field?" she asked me.

"Well", I replied, "for reasons similar to yours. But before I answer your question, I have to ask you why you chose personal training. Not necessarily fitness, but training other people."

"Oh yes, I forgot! When I get excited I just can't stop myself from being so open! I love helping people. I love watching them overcome their challenges, build that confidence, and just go for it! I love being a part of that! That's why personal training is my passion. I have no experience in it, but I think I can be good at it."

"And what makes you think you can be good at it?" Tank asked her.

Without skipping a beat, she answered "Because *you'll* teach me, Tank!" The Tank blushed. She got him—good.

"Ryan", Susan asked, "what is your definition of success for yourself in personal training?"

Susan knew what I was thinking, and she was way ahead of me. It was a question that we asked all of our candidates.

Ryan laughed nervously, then she answered "I'm...really not sure. I guess training lots of clients and making sure they get results. Right?"

Susan smiled at her and said "That's right, but you have to have a vision of success for yourself too. If you can develop that vision for others, don't you think you need one for yourself also?"

"Ryan, do you have a vision of success for yourself?" I asked.

She shifted side to side on the Swiss ball. For a moment, I was concerned she would fall off, but she kept herself on the ball. She bounced up and down for a second, which amused me momentarily, because I saw in that moment someone who wanted to play a simple game where there was no score, and no one needed to win. She wanted everyone to have fun, that was all. This was a good attitude, in the outset, but not helpful when challenges arise. As both Susan and Tank found, something had to drive them to overcome. And more often than not, the source of that drive was their vision.

"I guess...I don't really have a vision yet. Do I need one?" Ryan asked.

We all nodded in unison. "I can help you there, Ryan", Tank said. "I'm full of visions—ask anybody in the gym!" We all laughed, as we knew that Tank had grown into a mentor for all the new trainers. He was like a big brother to them at this point, and he seemed eager to take Ryan under his wing.

"Ryan", I said, "you need to listen to what I have to say."

"Yes sir", she replied.

"At first you won't be able to choose your clients. Sometimes your first client is at 5:30AM, and you will have to wake up at 4AM just to get here early enough to be ready for the session. At first it will seem like fun, but after weeks of this it can be challenging. There will come a point where no matter how much I pay you, no matter how much you love your client, when that alarm goes off, you're going to ask yourself if it is worth it to get up and train your client...or not. No amount of money, passion, ingrained habits, routine, nothing will get you to train that client, unless you have a vision of success for *yourself* that is so compelling and so captivating that nothing—*nothing*—will stop you. Do you understand?"

"Yes, I absolutely understand", she replied.

"Good", I said to her, "that is the first secret to becoming unstoppable."

DEVELOPING THE VISION

An achievable vision of your business has many components. First, it has to be a vision of success. Second, it has to embody your core values. Last, it must be personally moving and inspiring. These three components must be present because the challenges of creating a successful business will often discourage you. Whether those challenges come in the form of temporary setbacks, increased competition, or unexpected market-driven factors, you will find often that the need for financial success will not be enough to sustain what can be characterized as an Olympian effort to overcome what feels like insurmountable odds. There are those who believe that the innate stubbornness of the specific individual often drives the will to win, despite setbacks and challenges. In fact, those stubborn enough to succeed have a clear and inspiring vision of what that success looks like.

First of all, your vision must clearly illustrate success - the bolder and more dominant the success, the better. Timid vision elicits timid effort. You must see yourself on the floor of a gym, completely confident in your mastery of equipment and exercise, of communication and education, of client interaction and coaching. That is one vision of success. Another vision is for you to see your clients happy, successful, and feeling fulfilled. Another vision is for you to do this with an unequalled level of passion and fulfillment for the rest of your life. All of these visions start the process of creating an internal reality that you believe in, one that originates in the deepest part of who you are, and one that you will ultimately create as the reality of your surroundings.

Secondly, your vision must also embody your core values. It is important to see yourself as being passionate in your work, in delivering the highest level of quality that you are capable of, while at the same time expressing and developing your individuality as you continue to grow and succeed. By doing so, you start to bring your core values to life, in a way that permeates and affects your professional life and environment. You start to visualize in your mind's eye that your work is deeply tied to who you are, what you aspire to build, and who you ultimately want to become. Seeing yourself as a passionate fitness professional on the training floor, delivering the highest quality of programming and coaching, while continuing to encourage each individual client to their personal best brings to the forefront a very vivid illustration of what your definition of success will look like.

Lastly, if you have followed these two steps correctly, this vision (which is the foundation of your business) will greatly inspire you and urge you to action with a sense of purpose in your work, regardless of the challenges presented to you, while inspiring you to constantly grow and develop. Once this vision of success is clear, what you have is the essential foundation for your business: *a business purpose and strategy.*

THINKING STRATEGICALLY

Business strategy is often confused with business planning, but they are two very separate things.

Planning provides the structure within which you can operate efficiently; strategy gives direction and purpose to your efforts. There are many plans that promise a route to success, but only those with a clear direction *towards* success will bear fruit. A true strategy will always lead to the clear vision that you initially developed—a vision that always at the forefront of your mind and deeply felt in your heart. All your professional efforts and daily tasks must lead you towards the full realization of this vision.

For strategic thinkers, every thought and action must lead toward the fulfillment of the original vision. It requires us to implement the following:

- Every thought and action must lead toward the realization of this vision.
- All actions that do not lead to the realization of the vision must be discarded without hesitation.
- A plan must bring this vision more vividly into reality.
- Any plan that obstructs the clarity of this vision is also to be discarded without the slightest hesitation.

There is a word for this way of thinking: *obsession*. One sure way to guarantee the success of your business is simply to be obsessed with it. This means that any thought and action that even begins to dim the vision of your success, or make your work less engaging, must simply be removed from your scheme of self-management. Success or failure relies primarily on your ability to self-manage your vision of yourself, your ability to choose the correct thoughts and actions that elicit the desired results. The primary cause of your success is your ability to self-manage your thoughts, your words, and your actions. More significantly, the primary cause of failure is the inability to self-manage. The success of your business relies heavily upon your ability to manage yourself *first*. If you are not focused on your business, if it does not inspire you to live and breathe it, then you are in the wrong business. Pick something else to occupy your time.

At some point in their career, every personal trainer reaches several key points where their ability to choose the correct thought determines their level of success. If your client wants to train at 5:30AM, and you must get up at 3:30AM to get there early to provide the best service, the first thought that comes to mind will determine your action and decision. And if that thought is in any way connected to your vision of providing passion-driven training of the highest quality, if it is in any way connected to your vision of success for your business, then 3:30AM will not deter you in the slightest.

However, if you look simply at the facts of the scenario, without the aid of your clearly defined vision, you will (if only for a moment) hesitate to commit. That hesitation will carry over eventually into your ability not just to manage this particular client, but ultimately in how you manage your choices that either optimize your abilities or simply sabotage them. It then becomes a simple cost/benefit proposition—*is it worth getting up at 3:30AM to meet this client? Is the $100/$200/$500 an hour they are paying me worth the exchange in my quality of life?*

Without a strategy in place, the answer will be no. Not for $200, not for $2,000. You can raise your rates to whatever amount you want, but if your thoughts and subsequent action are not tied to a grander vision of success beyond monetary gain, success that is tied to your core values, to your identity, to the standards that you represent, no dollar amount will satisfy you. And no effort will be worth it. You will, at some point, give this client up—simply because your thoughts and actions were not determined by a clearly defined and inspiring vision that could have helped you to think and decide strategically.

It is for this reason that in order to become successful, it is important to ask a simple question that will help ensure each decision you commit to is tied to your strategy: "What does this have to do with my vision of success?" If it leads to a greater clarification or realization of that vision, commit to that decision 100%. If it does not, even if it vaguely dims your vision or sways you from what inspires you, discard that thought or action from your life. Absolutely nothing must stop you from driving your business to success.

This practice will also greatly increase your ability to start developing a plan to realize your success. Every strategic objective and deadline of your plan must lead towards the realization of that vision. The significance of this cannot be overstated, because it is very easy to clutter a plan with insignificant measurable and actionable tasks that ultimately lead nowhere. The primary measure of a successful plan is this: does it make your vision more *vivid*? If it does, it should be implemented. If it obstructs the vision, the plan is unacceptable, regardless of what success it promises to achieve.

THE MISSION STATEMENT

Once your core values have been established, you are ready to define your plan, commit it to paper, and launch it on its journey towards unpredictable reality. That reality starts with a mission statement. A mission statement has three essential components. It:

• States what the brand/company intends to do for its market/client
• States how the trainer will develop from the process
• States how the brand/company will be profitable and sustainable

The first statement essentially describes what you as the trainer plan to do for your clients. An example would be "To deliver the finest in performance-driven personal training by managing every aspect of the client's overall development." This states very clearly how the client will benefit by training with you.

The second statement describes how you plan to develop and grow. An example would be "Passion that is directed towards quality growth, to ensure that the fitness professional grows and exceeds potential year over year." This statement makes clear, both to you and your client, how dedicated you are to your craft. As important as it is to position your product and service so that they are exactly what your client needs, it is similarly important to make clear how your professional growth within your chosen craft should be equal to the growth and development of the clients that you serve.

Finally, it is important to understand how your clients and your professional growth are tied to the profitability of your business, so that your endeavors are sustainable year over year. Always remember that profitability is synonymous with sustainability. Of course you want to ensure that your primary focus is to help your clients achieve their goals. The best way to do that is by making your business profitable, so that you do not need to take on work outside of your chosen profession.

Let us closely examine the structure of this mission statement. The first statement relates to your intended market (your clients). The second statement relates to your product (your expertise). The last statement relates to your business's ability to deliver your product to your intended market so that it produces a level of profitability that makes it a sustainable business model.

I recommend that you read your mission statement on a daily basis, as a reminder of what you intend to do for your clients that day, how you intend to raise your efforts to a level that meets your professional standards, and lastly to ensure that your efforts are profitable. Familiarizing yourself with the statement that you have created will fill your tasks, objectives, schedules, and duties with a sense of galvanizing purpose. It helps connect your daily efforts to your vision of the future. By simply internalizing your mission statement, you are connecting what you are doing today with a set of long-term goals for the future. For our purposes, these long-term goals are called *strategic objectives*.

COMMITTING TO THE VISION

At this point, you have written out your core values, made vivid your vision of success, and defined your business purpose via a mission statement. None of this is new or innovative—what you are applying to your profession is a basic practice in running a business in any industry. Whether we are doctors, lawyers, investment bankers, architects, engineers, or restaurant owners, we all want to achieve a level of success that will give us financial independence to enjoy our lives, and a certain degree of fulfillment through the work that we do.

In order to make all of this come closer to reality, you must now bridge the gap between vision/strategy, and implementing a plan. Notice that in the process of identifying your core values/vision/ mission statement, there are no *measurable objectives* set in place. You have yet to create parameters that measure your ability to deliver quality, your business profitability, how your passion contributes to the success of your clients, or how your individuality is a key strength to be leveraged in your business. Creating a set of *strategic objectives* helps bridge that gap between internal reality and external realization. The vision that inspires you must now enter the world of business—and the way to do that is to look at what you can measure: the three components of your mission statement.

The first item addresses how much of your intended market you anticipate capturing by delivering on the services that you offer. These are your potential clients. In order to create a set of strategic objectives that will make this first statement measurable, ask yourself: How many clients am I training per day? How many clients am I training per week? How many times are they training? How many total clients do I have in my roster?

In most cases, your intended market is how many clients you intend to have in your roster, with a certain number of training sessions in mind. An example would be:

• **Strategic Objective #1:** 35 clients training an average of 3 times a week.

By defining your first strategic objective, you are now coming closer to making your vision real by making it achievable, and *anything* is achievable if it is measurable.

Your second strategic objective addresses your *product.* We don't offer tangible objects that sit on a shelf that we then give to our clients once a transaction is completed. You are offering a service, which requires a unique manner of delivering your product to help your clients achieve their goals. The product you are delivering, in many ways, is actually *you.* More specifically, your professional identity. The constant development and refinement of your professional identity is sometimes called your business acumen or "people skills". It is, however, a more in-depth process than you may initially assume. The development of your *professional identity* requires a constant and almost obsessive review of how your actions and communication style directly impact those around you. How you move, how you speak, the decisions that you make require a high-level of scrutiny in order for you to deliver on the service that you are promising—getting your clients in shape. Your clients will purchase your services for several reasons, but one very important reason is their trust in your ability to manage *yourself*. In other words, if you are aware of your body language, careful and selective in your choice of words, and have clear reasoning ability that makes your case sound and unassailable, more often than not the client will purchase your product because they believe that you are *trustworthy*.

Investing in honing your competency of technical expertise is one way of doing that, but the most effective way of being trustworthy is to refine your poise and demeanor as a leader in your field in addition to establishing your financial success. Your mission statement must address the consistent development of the people responsible for delivering your service, because they are the product that constitutes the quality of the overall offering. Along with your expertise in the field, you must develop and acquire the business and leadership skillsets that will set you apart from the rest.

- **Strategic Objective #2:** Each client will receive a minimum of 4 assessments per year, as well as a personalized program with face to face communication on a weekly basis, all customized to address the individual's needs with quality care and world-class customer service.

If we achieve strategic objective #1 (35 active clients), you will be organizing 140 assessments throughout the year, delivered with a sense of confidence, poise, and compassion—three qualities associated with effective leadership. This strategic objective alone will not only help you in managing the key metric of client retention, but it also gives you a separate directive: your education and development must move *beyond* the realm of technical expertise, and more towards the leadership and effective communication realms.

When you put the first two strategic objectives in place, not only will your customer service and sales competencies be put to the test, but you will also be pushed to educate yourself further in these realms to ensure a higher success rate in building your business.

The last statement puts the measure of profitability and sustainability to the test. As much as you are driven by passion and vision, your professional efforts must be measured by the level of profitability of your business. This statement *is your commitment* towards producing financial results. By doing so, you are pushing your abilities to deliver on these results, no matter what challenges lie ahead of you, no matter how difficult things get.

- **Strategic Objective #3:** Annual income will fall between $150k-$185k gross income (or whatever financial goal you set for yourself).

These three statements and their correlative strategic objectives start to put into place the next step in your business building phase: the planning phase.

THE LITTLE PROTÉGÉ

"I did it!"

At this point Susan and I were used to hearing Ryan regale us with another story of her success.

"I sold another package of sessions! She's my 10th client and *I love her!!!*" Ryan exclaimed.

"That's wonderful," I said to her. I gave her a high-five, and so did Susan. "Ryan, could you close the door? I think your 10th client might have heard you."

"Woops! I keep doing that!" she laughed.

Tank came into the office beaming with pride. "So how's my new star!? Ain't she something! My little protégé is the best! I taught her everything she knows. Especially that thing where you keep the office door open when you tell your managers you sold a package!"

Tank laughed and laughed and slapped his knee. As funny as it was, it was actually true. His voice would boom down the hallway like a loudspeaker whenever he sold a package. Deafening to this day.

"Tank, your little protégé is going to take your number one spot soon! How would you like that?" Ryan joked.

"I'd LOVE IT! It would be the BEST THING!" he smiled and laughed.

Ryan put her arms around the Tank, barely making it all the way around his barrel-chest. She buried her face in his chest, and through her muffled voice we heard "That's right you'll love it! I'll make you proud!"

As the laughter went around the office, my mind went back, momentarily, to a time when there was little happiness to be had at my division. There were other trainers then, different trainers. Some new, some veteran, all with the same hopes and dreams of Susan, Tank, and Ryan. Many of them couldn't muster the fortitude to weather the daily challenges, the constant rejection, the relentless pressure. Some simply needed to grow up and become successful adults first, before achieving any other form of success. Many of them left of their own accord. Some I had to fire. I never let any of them know that I would, in fact, feel a bitter pang at their departure. Whether they knew it or not, I believed in all of them. Nothing hurts more than seeing someone you believe in stop believing in themselves before they allowed the process to actually set in. Once they start not believing in themselves, they no longer believe in anything you say. They start viewing your encouragement as a form of manipulation or odd derangement.

Somehow, through those trying times, I found myself in an office full of mirth, where people shared a love for a profession, a passion for fitness, and a genuine admiration for each other. While Tank and Ryan were acting like a cute brother and sister act, I allowed myself a moment to reflect on what I was seeing. How truly rare it is, to be in such a place in one's professional development, that one can see the fruits of one's labor blossom right in front of your eyes. I could not believe my luck.

I could not believe the blessing. I decided, in that moment, to allow myself a small dose of happiness, to commemorate what I believe few managers in their entire professional careers may never experience—the happiness one feels very deeply when one's vision of success is realized by those he completely believed in, while no one else did. I could, for a moment, allow myself to feel this happiness, this sense of quiet accomplishment and redemption. Yet, as happy as the moment was, I simply could not help myself.

I wished Hal was there to share this moment with me. With all of us.

ON PLANNING

Planning is where most trainers excel—we generally deal with numbers: loads, reps, sets, grams, fluid ounces, percentages. This technical expertise skillset should cross over somewhat easily to the profitability and productivity planning of building a business. In many ways, it is an identical process.

The macrocycle goal for the fitness plan is similar to the strategic objective of the 3rd statement in a mission statement. There has to be a sense of an endgame and metric. And much like the strategic objective that you have set for your client in the macrocycle, the number must reflect a full realization of a much larger vision that, must be so clear in the mind's eye, that one is simply eager to get to the business of making it real. This is the power of creating a vision and mission statement—you will *want* to work, because your work has direction and purpose.

Planning requires focus and precision, with an overall desire to exceed. As much as your vision of success must inspire the trainer, it is limited because the picture does not fully detail the required steps necessary to achieve it. Planning does that by establishing the necessary steps towards realizing the vision. This requires a level of focus and precision so that mistakes do not take away precious time from achieving success.

THE TIMELINE

With your list of strategic objectives in hand, the first step is to establish a *timeline*. Without a timeline, strategic objectives will have little chance of truly achieving completion, because it will always be easier to say to oneself that "I have objectives", as opposed to saying "I have *achieved* my objective." It forces you to be creative and courageous when faced with setbacks. A business exists because it has a purpose—a product for an intended market. However, in order for a business to thrive, for it to have real impact and relevance, it must have objectives that exist not just to be completed but to be constantly exceeded. Strategic objectives, in this sense, are not end-points, but markers of excellence that one must strive to always exceed. For example, to have achieved a financial goal of $185,000 by end of year is a marker of success. To have achieved that goal two months ahead of time, allows you the opportunity to exceed their goal by 20%—a remarkable achievement because you beat your own forecast (in the double-digit category, no less). The power of this first step in planning, *establishing a timeline,* lies in giving you the ability to manipulate potential outcomes by calculating when *the objective will be achieved, not if it will be achieved.*

BACKWARD PASS TARGETING

Backward Pass Targeting simply means determining your short-term goals by planning backward. The value of this type of planning lies in its ability to give you complete mastery over its progress and implementation. You have total control. Using this technique achieves three things: One, the end is not a matter of if, but when and how you will achieve your final goal. Two, once success is a foregone conclusion, you have a sense of confidence as you proceed with implementing the master plan to fast-track its success. Third, with success within reach and your confidence boosted, you have a sense of control over the plan— even in the face of setbacks that, to most onlookers may seem daunting and discouraging.

For example, if you implement your plan in January, you have 12 months to achieve your goal of $185,000. That's a target of roughly $15,417 a month, give or take. A typical method of approaching these metrics is to position yourself in a way so that earning $15,416 a month must be consistently achieved. With consistent productivity, efficiency and effort, this method presumes that outcomes should be consistent and reliable. However, this does not take into consideration that business is driven and impacted greatly by the unpredictability of many different factors.

A typical setup for this approach goes like this:

- For January, February, and March, you expect to reach $15,417 on a regular basis.
- Because of travel and cancellations, your revenue in January is $13,322. You are technically *in the red $2,095*. Going forward, your new goal in February is now $17,512.
- February is worse, due to winter storms. Total revenue for the month is $11,345. You are in the red for February $4,071—down $6,165 for both January and February—and it is only the *beginning* of the year. For March, you have to deliver $21,584 in order to just stay on pace to hit the rest of the year.

Clearly this is a very stressful situation to be in—down 13% in the first two months of the year is stressful, considering that:

- Double-digits in the red in the beginning of the year.
- January and February tend to be strong months for sign-ups, so to be down 13% is a bad sign for the business overall.
- You are now supposed to deliver somewhere between $8k-$10k over your previous expectation, which is a number you have not hit before.

With these numbers, it's easy to talk yourself into a negative mindset. After all, how can someone exceed a number they have not hit before? How can they overcome a 13% deficit during what is supposed to be one of the strongest quarters of the year for sign-ups?

The problem here is not you, or that you missed a goal for the first two months. There are two essential problems with the way the plan was *set up*.

First: the plan was set up to achieve the overall goal via a consistent average revenue *per month*. $185,000 is the strategic objective; $15,417 is the projected target. Take the goal for the year ($185,000) and divide it by 12 months—which amounts to $15,417 monthly. The problem with this approach is that it does not allow *for variances in productivity,* which can affect the monthly goal. January generally has storms that affect travel, which affects member participation. Members tend to go on vacation as well. Without allowances for volatility, you are essentially set up for failure in the first two crucial months of the year. One could argue that consistent targeting is an effective way towards consistent productivity because it relies primarily on organization and compliance. However, life is unpredictable. Business is the discipline of managing and profiting *from unpredictability and volatility.* A plan that is destined for failure can be as easily constructed and consistently organized, just as a plan that is supposedly designed for success. Effective implementation of a plan that is going in the *direction* of failure will only make that plan highly efficient at failure. The ultimate success of a plan has little to do with the efficiency of its implementation, and more with its ability to maintain the vision of the original strategic objective and adhering to the original *direction and strategy.*

In other words—are you still set up to hit $185,000 for the year, even though you are down 13% in his first two months? The answer is YES.

- The direction of the plan is $185,000 for the year, but it is organized so that expectation is a monthly target of $15,417 per month. If we are looking at this from the perspective of being a planner, the trainer is already "off plan" by 13%/$6,165. However, if we are looking at this from the broader perspective of a strategist and leader, the plan can be modified.
- The strategist, involved primarily in achieving the strategic objective of hitting $185,000 for the year, must now ask—where can the other $6,165 be found in the next 10 months? The strategist

will backward pass the deficit *from the original goal, not forward pass it from the monthly deficit.*

Here is how backwards pass targeting can help you out of the red:

- By December, total revenue has to be $185,000. This is the touchstone, origin point, and final destination of the plan—every tactical shift has to be focused on this fixed point. No exceptions.
- This means by *June,* revenue should at minimum be $92,496: you have March, April, May, AND June to find $6,165. That's *four* months to make up the deficit, as opposed to traditional targeting where you are supposed to make up the deficit in one month. $6,165 in four months gives us an average of $1,541.25—roughly 10% over-performance per month between March and June.

This approach to planning allows you an ease of mind and confidence by allowing *flexible* implementation of planning and tactics, so that strategic objectives for the year and the overall vision remain achievable and fixed. This allows you to own the plan, not the other way around.

Another way to resolve this issue is to spread the deficit throughout the *remainder of the year*—an extra $616.50 per month until December.

An effective plan adheres to the direction of the original objective, but variances must be anticipated, and tactical shifts implemented throughout the year because the plan must succeed in achieving the overall goal. When a plan allows you to be flexible, innovative and creative by anticipating variances, you can create cushioning when times are bad. Most importantly, it allows boldness and daring when times are good; a plan must also inspire you to do more than is expected. In fact, a trainer, more often than not, will take risks and over-perform simply because innovation is now indelibly and measurably linked with achieving the original strategic objective. You work hard when times are bad, but you work harder when times are good, and productivity is on the upswing. If a plan is designed solely to be effective in achieving and measuring goals, but does not inspire or engage you in the process, the plan will fail. A plan, in the end, must be flexible enough for unpredictability and allow for you to decide the best route to achieve success.

Thoughts on
Targeting, Tactics, and Insight

View your designated targets as guideposts that lead you toward success. The tactics you implement, both on a daily and weekly basis, require innovation, creativity, and a taste for risk-taking. Planning creates a level of comfort because it lays out a consistent vision against the unpredictability and ebb and flow that is the very nature of business. To take this analogy further, we often refer to our plan as a "ground plan", but the nature of business is cyclical, like the ocean tides. Each wave is different, and each one requires a different tactic and approach.

Your plan is organized data that will help you make decisions that affect your business. You must not, however, make the mistake of confusing your plan with your *core business*. You are in the business of identifying a market for whom you can supply your product and service, and make a profit doing so. Do not make the mistake of thinking that you are in the business of *implementing a plan*; a plan can be designed by anyone who does not understand the business—in fact the best planners tend to be the ones who have *never* been in the business. It is important to constantly remind yourself that you have a mission statement to fulfill, not a plan to implement. Your targets will guide you towards your ultimate objectives, but they are only guideposts that indicate whether you are on track and going in the proper direction.

The difference between implementing a plan and achieving its subsequent targets, and a mission statement and going towards strategic objectives is that each one has a different, but distinctive and unique *mindset*. The planner is more oriented to organization, but can lose sight of purpose and vision. The strategist is more vision oriented, but requires a plan as a buffer that involves systems and controls. Considering the level of unpredictability that comes with the territory of being profitable in the fitness industry, the most effective approach is that of the strategist—one who is capable of riding wave upon wave undeterred. As a strategist, you must concern yourself less with consistency, and more with brilliance. You must concern yourself with analyzing and anticipating a constantly changing landscape, as opposed to busying yourself with investigations as to why your plans do not consistently deliver the intended results.

You must be insightful, analytical, organized when needed, but ready to break the rules when called for. When you think strategically, you understand and accept that any outcome is possible, so you prepare and plan for each and every outcome. Targets and tactics must be created, reconstructed, innovated, then revisited in order to constantly measure yourself against your previous efforts and the objectives you have set up for yourself.

Business is a not a checklist; it is the ability to thrive in unpredictability.

THE UNKINDEST CUT

"I just don't...understand." Ryan could only muster those words out of her, when we met on Sunday morning at my office. She had risen to the top very quickly, and had signed an impressive 27 clients by the time she had taken the number one spot. She was not only successful, she was well loved. Her teammates adored her, and her clients simply couldn't stop singing her praises.

Then, within a space of one week, 9 of her clients left her. 3 had to relocate, 2 needed surgery, and 1 lost his job. The other 3 gave no reasons at all. They just wanted to try something different. As her manager, I understood that these losses are a natural part of being in the fitness business. Clients come to you and train with you for their own reasons, and they leave for their own reasons.

She sat still in Susan's chair. Her breathing was steady, but shallow. Her eyebrows would furrow suddenly, then soften. She searched for an explanation.

"They were all doing so well. They were following their programs. They were getting better. Is this how it is?" She asked me.

"Is this how what is, Ryan?" I replied.

"Is this how I am supposed to feel after all the work I have done?" Her voice was a steady whisper, and it was growing as she started putting her thoughts together. "I gave so much to each one of them. I give everything to every session, every client, every rep, and they leave like it was nothing. Like it was all nothing."

"Ryan," I said, "I understand losing 33% of your client base is tough. I understand..."

Ryan rolled her chair toward me.

"One of my clients became my friend. She told me her problems. She told me her heartaches. I even attended her sister's wedding. So how can she just not come back? Not answer my emails? Is that how it goes? They just don't care, do they?"

She had me there. Even though I wanted to keep the conversation about her percentages and how to rebuild her business, Ryan had brought up something that even I myself had a difficult time dealing with: what do you do when you care about clients who don't care about you as a person? I could only tell her what I knew, what I felt.

"Ryan, I think that if they cared, they cared for you at the time, but only for that time. I don't know if anyone can care forever."

"Do you think they cared at all?" she asked.

"I'm sure all our clients do, as much as they can. Do you think she's as upset as you are right now?"

She started to put it together. Her eyes glanced at one of her reports. She scanned it for a moment, then she pushed the report away. I could see her fighting tears.

"Ryan, what do you think your client is doing, right now, while you're here upset? You're the only one who can fix this. I can help you, but I want you to see that this isn't always about them. It has to be about you too."

"Okay, I think I get it. What are my numbers?" Ryan replied.

"You're down. Your numbers don't lie. People often feel they need to lie, but your numbers will never lie to you. They hurt sometimes, but they don't lie. And that, in itself, is its own strange comfort."

"I'll do my best to bounce back. That's all I can do, right? My best?"

"It's all anyone can do Ryan." She looked at her report, and at this point I started to feel that she was starting to understand what this is really all about.

THE 4 BUSINESS MODELS AND STRATEGIES OF PERSONAL TRAINING

Like all things, a business goes through phases of growth, and you must understand that there is a difference between managing and growing a business as opposed to going to a job. Jobs do not necessarily require the level of investment and added skillsets that are called for in managing a business. Personal training is not a job, where once you apply, interview, you are then subsequently offered the position. Personal training does not afford you a guaranteed salary or insurance benefits.

Once you have created your business, you must now manage and grow that business. Each phase of the process requires a specific strategy. It is important to reiterate here that you are not approaching this from the mindset of planning but of strategy. One of the limitations of the planning mindset is that it does not account for anticipated setbacks or challenges and how that can affect growth. Stress-runs and data analyses can do that, but a strategic mindset allows not only for fluctuations in both productivity and market shifts, it also allows for the necessary shifts as one overcomes these challenges and moves toward eventual success.

You cannot expect to lift 250 pounds the same way one would lift 25 pounds. This comparison, though simplistic, is a clear illustration of how one's business strategy and management approaches evolve from managing 25 clients to 250 clients.

The 4 Business Models of Personal Training are:

- Startup
- Breakout
- Solid
- Critical Mass

Each model requires a specific strategy with specific targets. Each model requires a dramatic shift that has to be anticipated. Take careful note that each model is not defined as a level of performance: do not look at a Startup as a model that failed to achieve Critical Mass metrics—each model's success and failure is measured by how successfully it actualizes the *strategy* that is appropriate for that specific model. You cannot compare a new lifter to a veteran lifter—they are two different people with different goals (and sets of predictable setbacks). Similarly, you cannot compare one model to another—one is not necessarily more successful than another. You can say one is more profitable and fiscally feasible than the other, but those are not our sole measures of success. You must clearly understand and study the strategies of each model, so that you can master each one in order to successfully transition into the next.

RELEVANT AND ASSOCIATED METRICS

How much can you expect to earn by becoming a personal trainer? $35k? $60k? $90k? $175k? Your decisions are often shaped by a singular metric—your annual income, but this is the mindset of an employee who sees personal training as a job. However, as a fitness professional who is tasked to manage and grow a business, you must concern yourself not only with your annual income, but the relevant and associated metrics that ultimately contribute to the revenue you desire. This differentiation in mindset, between the singular metric and the multi-metric approach, is important to define because our strategies, plans, and related tactical implementation (all requirements when it comes to managing a business) may be disorganized if we are ultimately seduced by the singular metric approach, which is the mindset of an employee.

For example:

A candidate for a personal training position is looking to enter the fitness industry because his current job does not allow him the freedom to indulge in his true passion—working out. His current salary is $60,000, which includes medical benefits, but his love for fitness is the prime lure to personal training. He is willing to start at the bottom to make a career change.

An added lure is the potential to make his own hours, which allows him a greater opportunity for determining appropriate work-life balance ratio. To top it all off, he read that a personal trainer made $60,000 *in one month* by implementing an aggressive marketing system that boosted their sales capacity.

The primary metric that seems to attract this particular candidate is the potential for earnings growth for *less labor*. The attraction of earning $60,000 in one month is very powerful—how can you resist a position that will give you the opportunity to earn in one month what formerly took you one year to make?

Is it possible to bring in $60,000 in one month? The answer is yes. What makes those of us who are veterans of the profession less optimistic is not that it is not achievable, but that the perspective only takes into account one vantage point (that of an employee) and one metric (that which is associated with annual income). The error in this approach comes from viewing only this single metric as relevant, without taking into consideration the multiple associated metrics that can lead to variances, setbacks, and challenges a trainer faces.

If we are to examine this more closely, we must ask questions about the associated metrics of the relevant and alluring metric: earning $60,000 in one month.

When Revenue Is Not Revenue

Although questions about variable and fixed costs can apply here, they are outside of the scope of this book, and can be addressed by a more standard business approach. The questions we will ask are specific to our industry and our business, as that is that is our focus here.

- How many sessions were sold?
- How many clients bought these sessions?
- How much is each session?
- How many times a month, on average, is each client training?

Each question is related to an associated metric. The first is associated with inventory (the number of sessions purchased for the month); the second with client roster (the number of clients you are training for the $60k you were paid); the third with the trainer's average revenue (how much money is the trainer being paid per session), and the fourth question with throughput (the rate at which inventory is used, so that the client renews and pays for more inventory).

So far, based on our line of questioning, *four associated metrics* (inventory, client roster, average revenue, and throughput) correlate directly with the value of $60k in one month. We must approach each one of these as a variable that can determine the ultimate value of "$60,000 in one month".

Why is it important to determine the ultimate value of this relevant metric? Because we need to understand if this $60,000 *is repeatable* month over month, or if it is their total income for the year. Similar to hearing someone can bench press 550 pounds, we can understand the value of an athlete's strength based on several *associated* metrics:

- Can they bench that weight every day? Or once a year?
- Do they weigh 300 pounds? Or 150 pounds?
- Are they in powerlifting gear? Or are they raw and natural lifters?

We cannot completely understand the value of a metric until we understand the full context within which that metric was achieved. For our business purposes, we will concern ourselves primarily with managing associated metrics with the relevant metric.

Here are some scenarios:

- Did the trainer sell one session to one client for $60,000?
- Did the trainer sell 60,000 sessions to 60,000 clients for $1 each?

If it is the former, there is a high probability that this client will train, at the very *minimum*, once a month for 12 months and gross annual income comes out to $720,000. If it is the latter scenario, this trainer will be training every client, for every hour of every day, non-stop, for the next 6.8 years. The reality will of course fall widely between the two extremes, but it is important to illustrate how each associated metric can determine the ultimate value of the initial amount. The former obviously offers greater value, whereas the latter is a virtual impossibility. Thus it is important for us to identify the dynamics between the associated metrics of our business so that our efforts are accurately reflected in our relevant metrics: productivity, and profitability.

Let us take a look again at our $60,000 a month model, this time looking at a more realistic scenario:

- Client Roster: 30 clients
- Number of sessions: 30 each

By examining these associated metrics we can surmise that each client bought a package of 30 sessions for a price of $2,000. (30 clients x 30 sessions = 900 total sessions in *inventory*); ($60,000 divided by 900 sessions = $66.67 *average revenue*); ($66.67 x 30 sessions = $2,000 for a package of 30 sessions).

The unpredictability and variability arises when we look at the associated metric of throughput—the rate at which inventory (their sessions) go through the actual business. If your throughput is relatively high, you have a very high probability of making another $60,000 next month, because your clients have to renew their package of sessions. If your throughput is low, you may not see $60,000 for another year.

- In order for your client roster to renew their sessions in the following month, they have to have used all 900 sessions in 30 days. Since each client has 30 sessions, each client has to train *seven days a week*.
- In order for you to make $60,000 a month, for an annual income of $720,000, your business throughput must be 30 sessions a month *per client*. In other words, your business has to have 30 clients training every day.

This may sound manageable on paper, but there is something else to consider: your time is a limited resource. Money, to a certain extent, is a renewable resource, but time is not. In order to make this a feasible proposition, you have to train 3 clients at a time, for 10 hours straight, every day.

$60,000 in a month sounds wonderful, but an analysis of the cost to benefit ratio clearly reveals that most people would not consider the effort worthy of the amount, because of the substantial cost to quality of life (and health) that it entails.

The purpose of this numbers-heavy exercise is to illustrate the dynamics at play when managing and growing a business. The associated metrics listed are but a few of the ones that we can investigate and leverage, although these are not the only metrics that contribute to the overall performance of a business model. As managers of a business and leaders in our field, it is important for us to keep an eye on the prize, which is the strategic objective, while we are similarly in touch with the associated metrics that ultimately determine the value of our professional efforts.

THE LEVER PRINCIPLE

A lever is an associated metric that can determine the level of performance of a business at any given time.

A relevant metric, such as profitability or productivity, is thrilling when all exceed our expectations. Nothing can beat that feeling of winning, consistently. There is nothing worse than the dread feeling of failing, and that there is no way to reverse the course, especially when total revenue is far lower than earlier forecasts.

In one of our earlier examples, the goal of $185,000 by EOY December seemed achievable by spreading the incurred deficit throughout the remainder of the fiscal year. Achievable in theory, especially because that plan was set in place in March, which gave the trainer a 10 month cushion to achieve or over-perform. That is one scenario, and it is a very hopeful one.

The plan becomes almost totally unrealistic if the scenario changes—it is now October. Spreading the deficit went from a 10 month span to a 3 month span—a 70% reduction in month-over-month spread, which raises concerns and stress levels for a trainer who may miss their goal, with a shorter window of opportunity and a smaller margin for error.

A plan or tactic can only be deemed effective if it adapts itself successfully to the present circumstances and addresses the specific challenges that a particular situation offers. In our example, the effectiveness of a plan implemented in March is all but neutralized if implemented in October. Time constraints aside, there are direct-market factors that contribute to raising the level of the setbacks—with holiday season around the corner, member sign-ups tend to drop because they are spending money on holiday gifts and cutting back on personal luxuries. More often than not, personal training tends to be classified as a personal luxury.

A plan that addresses this setback is required and needs to be immediately implemented. Before setting up a plan, insight and analysis must be set up. Without these two in place, you might as well set up the March plan for October, with the rationale that since it was effective then, it should be similarly effective now. What you must review and analyze are our associated metrics, in order to determine which one you are going to leverage as the spearhead of our tactical shift; the one number, which, if improved drastically, can turn the entire business quickly and definitively towards the direction of success. This number is the lever.

It is important to discipline yourself to identifying just *one* lever, rather than implement a scatter-shot approach in the hopes of an overall improvement. Your potential client may request that they lose 15 pounds, become toned, and be able to complete a triathlon, but you do not build a program that addresses each request *simultaneously*. Bear this in mind, as you read an analysis of a business model and their associated metrics, in the hopes of identifying the lever.

The trainer who once produced $60,000 in a month made a change in his current model, so that his work-life balance would not be so negatively affected, with a goal of "$60,000 worth of *sales* in one month", as opposed to "$60,000 of *income* in one month". It was a more manageable and achievable target if the trainer viewed the $60,000 as a sales metric, which would be collected once his services have been rendered (i.e. trained them). Smart move, because it then allowed him to realistically budget his income as

$15,000 a month. Each client trained about 7.5 times a month, with each session worth $67. He was still working pretty hard—about 11 clients a day, 5 days a week—but now he has weekends to spend relaxing and enjoying life. His gross annual income will come out to about $180,000, since clients renew every 4 months or so.

Take your time to read this paragraph several times—this is a typical schedule for a very busy but successful personal trainer.

Here is the strategic objective: $180,000 by end of year.

Associated metrics are as follows:

- 30 clients on his roster
- Average revenue: $67/session
- Throughput: 7.5 sessions a month
- Inventory: 30 sessions/4 months/per client

Each associated metric and their dynamics contributes to the achievement of our trainer's strategic objective for the year—$180,000.

Then, seemingly from out of nowhere, the scenario changes:

About 7 of this trainer's clients have to skip out of town beginning in June, and will return in September. Their reasons vary: travel, work, family, medical reasons, and taking a break from training. As part of our customer care model, it is important that we take into consideration the reasons for their departure, and include it as part of the relative data that we compile as part of their history. However, since we are looking at managing our business, their reasons have little impact on the matter at hand: this trainer has taken a 23% hit in their client roster for the next 3 months, and a near 24% hit in monthly revenue, which is now down from $15,000 a month to $11,482.50. This year's projected earnings is now down from $180,000 to about $169,000.

For many veteran trainers, this is a common scenario, as summer tends to be a slow season for personal training and gyms in general.

Despite the fact that this situation is not uncommon, it does raise other concerns, particularly if the trend continues.

- What if these 7 clients do not return in September as promised? What if they return in January? Or not at all?
- What if *7 more* clients leave?
- Are there outside economic factors that are affecting the market across the entire industry, so that indices are down across the board?
- Is there a system in place to mitigate any of these potential outcomes, to reduce the current attrition rate?

There are several ways to answer these questions, but as you can see once we explore some of them, other metrics come into play that are outside of the scope of the book. Let us concentrate on the key associated metrics that directly impact this particular business, rather than speculate on potential economic and market-driven factors that may affect the downturn but not reverse the trend.

Let us examine again the associated metrics of this trainer's business:

- 23 clients on his roster (down from 30)
- Average revenue: $67/session
- Throughput: 7.5 sessions a month
- Inventory: 30 sessions/4 months/per client

The monthly target is $15,000, but with his client roster down, the trainer will not be reaching that target, so he needs to leverage one metric to make up the difference. Here are his options:

Client roster—get 7 new clients to fill the missing spots. This is possible, but there are some uncontrolled variables. Does the trainer have access to 7 potential clients? Will the trainer have the spots available for these 7 clients, even if/when the other clients return? Will they be training at the appropriate throughput, so that they are making up the difference in revenue?

Average revenue—raise average revenue in order to make up the difference. This is a popular notion among trainers, especially when they take a substantial hit in client roster, productivity, and overall revenue. "Raise your rates" is a very common piece of advice, because it promises lower client count and lowered throughput, but higher returns. There are, technically, fewer variables involved that could complicate other metrics such as inventory, throughput, scheduling, and work hours.

This trainer could potentially *double* his rate to $135 an hour, and cut the client roster in half, reducing his workload by 50%, working only 6 hours for 5 days a week, and still have weekends. With each client training 7.5 times a month for $135, gross monthly income comes out to about $15,075. Very attractive, but there are certain risks. The most concerning is this: what if 7 clients go on vacation again the following year, at the same time? What do we do—raise the rates again?

That is a 46% dip in business on a readily predictable and observable trend across markets, with a 47% dip in revenue.

The problem that raising rates presents is that it is difficult to ensure against an initial attrition in your client base, with an accompanying cost of time to rebuild. As attractive as the solution sounds, it creates its own problems at first. It also does not address the problem at hand, which requires a relatively quick turnaround.

Inventory—increase current inventory so that you have short-end cash to make up the difference. Certainly the trainer can have their current clients buy more sessions, so that sales stream can somehow be converted to revenue stream. The problem with this approach is that the trainer is now collecting on sessions that have yet to be completed, which will result in a negative net result when it comes time to use those sessions.

If this trainer asks 3 clients to pay $1,000 each in sessions in order to offset losses in income, the trainer essentially *owes* each client 15 sessions, totaling 45 hours altogether. Additionally, those 45 hours may count towards productivity and throughput, but revenue will have dropped because they had been applied to previous months. The result, for all this work, is the same.

Throughput: increase throughput. Essentially, this trainer is asking clients to train more. With an average throughput of 7.5 sessions a month per client, each of the 23 clients has to train about 10 times a month—an additional 2.5 times over the next 3 months.

This is the more successful route because the trainer is not adding additional costs or risking any resources in order to offset the loss in income. 2.5 more sessions per month per client is roughly an extra session every 3 weeks for the next 3 months. The proposition becomes even more interesting because this is one associated metric where the trainer can leverage a separate competency: technical expertise. The trainer can position an increase in training as beneficial to the client based on their knowledge that training frequency is correlated to elevated caloric output. The client will then view your recommendation as something beneficial to them, which increases the chances of it succeeding in convincing them.

By identifying the appropriate lever through a thorough analysis of the associated metrics that impact the achievement of the strategic objective, the trainer has a task and a focus. Failing is a part of achieving success, and there is little that can be learned from it. You must simply observe the failure, then find a way to mitigate any lasting effects that it may have. In this case the loss of 7 clients was unavoidable, but in the end it can be salvaged because of a simple analysis of the metrics that the trainer does have control over. The calmness you display when your business takes a substantial hit can be observed as a quality of leadership. Critical thinking and analysis do not come to those with a reactive mindset, which can occur when one is too busy implementing a plan. They are the attributes of the strategist and leader who has the capacity to see beyond the immediate situation.

THE FIRST BUSINESS MODEL: THE STARTUP

The Startup model of personal training is, in many ways, the most exciting and educational of all the business models. Starting from the ground up, there is little cost and risk, and all upside from practically every effort. It is a very good time to implement the P.A.C.T./Customer Care model in every interaction, and offer your assessment as a product sampler. Whether you are doing this on a gym floor or on your website, the key is to combine P.A.C.T. with the assessment offer.

The other key advantage of being a startup is that you are completely new to the market. The common wisdom is that it is important to establish credibility through experience and education, and not necessarily highlight your newness to the field. However, one particular advantage of being new is that you can put a lot of energy and excitement into the process of every interaction without necessarily having to manage tasks such as client retention and program management that veterans of the business may need to deal with. The primary characteristic of a startup model is that it is new, and with this newness comes excitement and energy.

STRATEGIC OBJECTIVES OF A STARTUP:

Strategy: Marketing

Strategic Objective: Acquisition of new clients up to 60% of total client roster target

If your goal is 30 clients on your roster, you are a startup until your roster is at 18 clients. The primary associated metric that you will be leveraging is the acquisition of clients for your roster.

The primary strategy of the startup model is a marketing model—get the word out and build your brand by simply implementing P.A.C.T. and offering assessments. Your intended market must know you exist before they can start to identify the needs that your product and service may be able to fulfill for them.

If you are a new trainer on a gym floor, implementing P.A.C.T. alone will get everyone buzzing about you. If you are a freelance trainer, it is important to include some form of P.A.C.T. in your electronic communication, if only to bring a heightened awareness of your presence in the market. You are open for business, and you should not be shy about it.

As you are acquiring new clients, do not be particular about the client's session frequency or even the time of day they wish to train. Your target is to acquire 18 clients—you can worry about throughput and average revenue at a later date. Some trainers make the mistake of adding qualifiers to this goal by being particular about the level of the potential client's commitment, even going so far as to see if their personality matches up with their clients. At this point, you cannot be that selective. Your focus should be on your startup strategy—*get new clients.*

Remind yourself that total revenue, return on investment, average revenue, or any other key operating indicators cannot be addressed at this point, for the simple reason that any investment of energy or effort into managing these metrics will give you little in return. The beauty, fun, and excitement of this particular model is that, for the time that you are here, you only need to manage *one* objective that is intimately tied to one strategy. You will have more than enough to worry about once your business has grown substantially.

THE BREAKOUT MODEL

Strategy: Roster Segmentation

Strategic Objective: 50% of your client base trains 8-12 times a month.

There is a reason why this is called the breakout model—you cannot stay in this model for long. If you do, you will not be able to maximize your efforts and your returns. In this model, several metrics need to be closely watched, and more importantly, the relationship of each metric *to each other* needs to be closely monitored. Improvement in one may actually create inefficiency or outright loss of productivity in another.

Let us examine this scenario *very* closely:

The trainer has 17 clients. He trains 5 clients a day, working 4 days a week. Each session costs about $100, but clients receive a discount of 25% if they buy a package of 5; 40% if they buy a package of 10. With these offers, roughly 9 of the trainer's clients purchased the 10 pack of sessions. 5 bought the 5 pack of sessions. 2 bought individually. Seems like the trainer is doing well, but he wants to increase total revenue while keeping the *same schedule*. What should he do?

This is a very common scenario among trainers who want to make more money. They want to show that their efforts are making a worthwhile profit not only for themselves, but to those who are close to them and perhaps also to their colleagues. In addition, a life event may create the necessity for greater return while keeping a sense of stability. Their overall goal is to somehow maintain current productivity while maximizing profits.

Compare this particular scenario to that of the trainer who had a more straightforward approach: to get more clients. This strategy may no longer be a viable option for the trainer because adding a client may also disrupt his schedule. However, he wants an increase in total revenue.

The breakout model creates this particular dilemma because the trainer does not have a revenue problem—he has a *strategic* problem. The initial strategy brought success, but continued implementation of that same strategy will now bring about a level of unwanted effort that may, in the long run, bring on a *perceived* level of diminishing returns. There are several ways to approach this dilemma but in the long run the simplest solution is not how he changes his focus on a particular metric; it is a matter of changing models and changing strategies.

- The trainer's overall session productivity is 5 sessions a day, 4 days a week. That is 20 sessions a week, with about 95-100 sessions on any given month.
- Total session inventory is 115 sessions.
- The two clients who purchase individually train, on average, about 6 times a month.
- Total sales is $2,140.

All of these metrics can be managed in conjunction with each other. What makes the process difficult is that the trainer in this scenario is insisting upon keeping the same schedule in order to implement the same *strategy*: startup.

If the trainer makes the appropriate change in strategy, it will become obvious that he can get to his goal simply by adding *another day*. This will exponentially increase his productivity while opening himself up to more opportunities. Once the shift in strategy has been created, it then becomes possible for the trainer to start sifting through his clients and start the process of *roster segmentation*: dividing up the client roster into 3 categories that will allow the trainer to leverage the best business opportunities, while incentivizing the rest to higher levels of session frequency.

Group 1:   Integral (8UP)
Group 2:   Fluctuators (8DOWN)
Group 3:   Under Median

8UP clients are clients who consistently train with the trainer twice a week or more; they have accepted training as part of their lifestyle. The 8Down clients are not the most consistent, but may still have bought in to the program, the trainer's expertise, and the overall process of keeping an active lifestyle that involves training. The Under Median group is the group that trains below the trainer's median. If the trainer's monthly productivity of 95-100 sessions is divided by 17 active clients, the average productivity of each client is somewhere between 5.5-5.8 sessions per month.

As a startup, it wasn't necessary to implement the client segmentation approach, because there wasn't a big enough client roster. If you have two clients, and they both train only 5 times a month, your job is not necessarily to incentivize them to higher levels of engagement. You are probably better off adding more clients, because if your approach for higher incentivizing fails, you could lose 50%-100% of your client roster. However, if you continue to focus on increasing your client roster as opposed to segmenting it, you can mitigate any losses by the volume of clients and their participation. In other words, if those two previous clients quit because you advised them to train more, the loss doesn't impact you as much because you have 15 other clients to make up for any losses.

However, once that client base is established, it is important to segment your roster, for a very simple reason: you must reserve time for clients who train *the most*. Clients who want to train three times a week at 7am will impact your relevant metrics more significantly than the client who trains twice a week at the same time. This is an important point: because most trainers think like an expert rather than a business owner, they have a hard time differentiating between clients who are getting results vs. clients who are *giving* them results. This ability to differentiate between the two requires us to think from a business owner mindset, as opposed to that of the technical expert. *The client must get their results by giving us results as well.* If the twice a week client can be incentivized to go to three times a week, that client can impact your breakout strategy more significantly. By segmenting your client roster, you now have the ability to approach the appropriate clients with a specific end in mind. Generally, the 8UP clients are praised for doing well. The 8DOWN are the clients who need extra care by listening to what could be holding them back from higher levels of participation and engagement. The Under Median group are the easiest group to either leverage or refer out to another trainer once you have acquired *new clients to replace their time slot*. At this point, you can be more selective in getting new clients by applying the simple criteria of whether the new client fits into the 8UP or 8DOWN group. By adding new clients who will train more, you can afford to either maintain or even reduce your total client roster count, because the new client's productivity makes up the difference.

This model is called the breakout model because you must "breakout" of the startup model of simply managing one metric (i.e. new clients), and must now start managing two—new clients along with increasing productivity by segmenting your client roster. This is the point where the trainer has to start thinking more like a business owner, along with being an expert.

SOLID MODEL

Strategy: Optimize Profit Per Session

**Objective: Increase hourly rate in conjunction with
        desired revenue per session**

The Solid Model is the next benchmark in your plan for growth. By this time, you have implemented the two-prong target approach of the Breakout Model—get new clients while segmenting the roster to increase overall productivity. By successfully implementing the breakout model, you should have achieved:

- An acceptable level of productivity: the trainer feels comfortable with their schedule and their hours.
- An acceptable level of profitability: the trainer is comfortable with the money that they are currently making from their current productivity.

This is a victorious moment, because you can now consider yourself successful at your profession. With the relevant metrics of productivity and profitability achieved, the business of this particular trainer can be said to have foundations in "solid" business practices.

The primary strategy in this model is to manage the average revenue on a per session basis. There are several criteria to take into account. You must closely manage this particular metric at this point, because building your business may have included three common industry practices:

• "Special discounted rates" due to low productivity/client count
• Complimentary sessions given for customer service reasons

A trainer may charge $200 an hour, but with these common practices they could in fact reduce the average revenue per session to as low as $90 for the same amount of work. Managing revenue on a per session basis is critical to effectively growing a business, because it is easy to confuse an increase in gross revenue with an increase in profitability and efficiency.

Here is an example of what happens when revenue *per session* is not managed, because there is too much focus on gross revenue:

• One trainer sells roughly $200,000 worth of sessions in 6 months. That's $33,333 a month for six months.
• Another trainer sells roughly $200,000 worth of sessions in the same amount of time, making roughly the same amount of money.
• The difference between the two is that one is working 14-hour days, 7 days a week. The other is working roughly 10 hours a day, 5 days a week.

As you can see, both trainers are making the same amount of money—$200,000 in 6 months is very respectable. But one trainer is working *more hours and more days*. The difference is that one trainer has an average revenue per session of $167, while the other has an average revenue of $80 per session. One can certainly argue that the second trainer should raise the per session rate. Though it is an important observation, and part of the overall equation, it is also essential to monitor on a regular basis how revenue per session fluctuates, depending on how one implements the 3 common practices that can affect that metric (discounts, specials, and customer service management). As much as trainers want to say that their hourly rate is fixed, it does not reflect the actual session rate when discounts are applied.

By the time you are at a solid level, there are several key practices that can ensure your continued success:

- Raising hourly rates
- Reducing the number of "specials"
- Keeping roughly 70%-80% of client roster at the 8UP category

It is at this point that you can consider yourself a success at what you are doing because you have reached a level of productivity that is sustainable, while making a comfortable living as a trainer. Most importantly, your client roster is made up primarily of "solid" clients who belong in the 8UP category.

Savor this particular benchmark in your professional career, because this is what winning feels like. Revel in it as much as possible, because the nature of the business of client-facing services is essentially cyclical. Success comes and goes not because we are unable to sustain it, but because the very essence of success is to be able to adapt with the fluctuations that occur in life.

THE CRITICAL MASS MODEL

Strategy: Optimize revenue per session/acquire new clients

Objective: Add new clients to the roster while maintaining optimal revenue per session

As I've said before, the nature of the training business is cyclical. Clients tend to come and go due to reasons beyond your control. Although you can program and deliver results at the highest level, life changes will occur that can impact your business directly. Clients may move because of a promotion, or a loved one may become ill, forcing them to take time away from their training. Even so, you can still prepare for these changes that can (if not anticipated) adversely affect our productivity and profitability.

The Critical Mass Model brings you back to your roots: acquiring new clients while optimizing your current revenue per session. This particular strategy is designed to offset any particular losses in session productivity due to fluctuations in the business cycle. It is relatively easy to predict which months clients will travel due to holidays and travel season, depending on your geographic location. During periods when session productivity can be low, it is important to start acquiring clients to fill up any empty slots that can be readily predicted.

The difference between the startup strategy of acquiring new clients versus the critical mass strategy comes down to how the new batch of new clients will fit into your current roster of clients. In the critical mass phase, new clients that are brought into the roster can be placed into two categories:

- Seasonal: new clients in this category can be brought into your schedule to increase your productivity without disrupting revenue because they are being brought in after you have increased your rates. Since they are seasonal, you should be able to convince them (with relative ease) to increase session frequency in order to maximize their results. However, if this strategy does not work, but they still want to train, you can still afford to bring them into your roster as a seasonal client, because you know that their time with you will end at a particular time of the year.
- New Integrals: a new integral client can greatly affect your overall productivity and average revenue because they will be part of your integral roster of clients. Be mindful, however, that although they are integral by definition (consistent session frequency while maintaining average revenue), only time will tell if they are truly part of the integral roster.

By categorizing new clients as either seasonal or new integral, you can more easily manage your forecasts for revenue and adjusting targets based on how many of them you acquire, and how they affect your productivity and profitability metrics. For example, if you have 5 new seasonal clients, and expect all 5 to leave at the end of 2nd quarter fiscal year, you can create productivity and profitability projections based on how you have managed the program for each one of them. The goal with seasonal clients is not to turn them into integrals—it is to maximize their session participation *before they eventually leave.*

Having seasonals as part of your critical mass roster helps you identify and acquire new integrals with a sense calm and deliberation, because the initial group is maximizing your productivity as a cushion against potential setbacks. 4 new integrals a year is a 24% growth in integral client roster—a double-digit increase in productivity and profitability. A seasonal roster allows you the luxury of time to acquire these 4 throughout the year.

THE 4 BUSINESS MODEL CONTINUUM

Success, like progress in physical fitness, is not linear. It is a path that is made up of small wins, a few setbacks, and more wins, and requires implementing tactics that minimize losses during anticipated downturns. Be mindful of this continuum as you invest more and more of your time in this particular field, because it will prepare you for the unending fluctuations that occur on a constant basis. For those of you who commit yourself fully to this profession, and remain determined to persevere through the challenges and obstacles, much of what will motivate you is the achievement of your strategic objectives for the fiscal year. Much of what will drive you will be the small but significant wins that accrue slowly with time, which suddenly switches you to the next business model then the next. Perhaps your achievement of Solid or Critical Mass may arrive in 6 months, or maybe even less. Once you achieve the business model you have been seeking, and complete the strategic objectives you have set out to achieve, you must celebrate the moment of victory. Remember that feeling of completion and winning, because that memory will be your touchstone when the true test of your will occurs.

That test will come in the form of fluctuation—and it will challenge your critical thinking, your analytical abilities, your self control, your professional identity, and to a certain extent your sense of reality. It may all sound very dramatic and like a business nightmare, but nonetheless anticipating fluctuation is what tests our mastery of our skill-sets. Anybody can complete a task. Anyone can achieve a goal. Anyone can win—once. It takes a very special and in-depth understanding of your skills and abilities when your victory is challenged by randomness and uncertainty.

With a roster consisting of 27 clients, 90% of which are integral, you may feel that success has been established and your business will continue to flourish for as long as you follow the same processes and complete the same tasks that brought you to this point. Then, seemingly out of nowhere, 7 integrals drop from the roster—a combination of relocations, illness, and layoffs completely take them out of the line-up. Follow that with 3 more who are dropping out for the next 4 months due to injuries that need surgery. With a total of 10 integrals out of the lineup, productivity and revenue will drop 33%.

This is a very drastic situation, but not outside of the realm of reality. It can happen to you, even if you are delivering the absolute best in terms of product, service, and results—fluctuations occur, and the truth is that they are at the very core of what we do. We rely on fluctuations for our clients to achieve their results, as well as our own, so it is only a matter of time for them to occur in a way that challenges our sense of confidence and proficiency.

When a personal trainer's business takes a substantial hit, their default assumption is often that they are not good at their profession, and what most trainers will do is to try and regain immediate control by managing their technical expertise. They believe that if they had more education in the technical expertise skill-set, the client would somehow still be training with them, the way they have done in the past. With further education, they believe they can start to market and advertise new and innovative offerings, in the hopes of attracting new clients and filling the vacant slots.

In this situation there are several perilous consequences to this line of thinking, simply for one primary reason: the trainer is viewing the situation from the perspective of finding immediate solutions. A dramatic drop in the number of clients will often elicit this particular response, but the peril of a wrong response lies in a trainer's inability to identify and understand the actual problem. And it is important to see the problem first.

With a 33% drop in integral client roster, and foreseeable drops in productivity and profitability, which *business model* are you in now?

If you can think this way, you'll find that the problem is not what you should do differently, but rather what you should implement based on your current productivity and its concurrent business model. This is, perhaps, the only time in a business's lifespan where a *strategic shift* is required in order to accommodate the new reality of the environment. In other words, if you find yourself falling from a Critical Mass Model in terms of productivity to a Breakout Model, your immediate plan should be to implement the Breakout Model strategy. This will allow you to recover quickly because you have previously implemented this strategy with measurable success, which led you to Solid and Critical Mass Business Models. This mindset will not only give you the confidence for a speedy recovery, it will help you anticipate the next steps and strategic shifts as you succeed.

Success requires the understanding that business, fitness, and life in general are essentially unpredictable, and that it is possible to offset even massive losses with the ability to take advantage of these waves of events as opportunities if we remain analytical and calm.

We tend to mistake unpredictability with danger, when in fact most dangers tend to be predictable and relatively easy to plan for. However, when we buy into the belief that unpredictability is the enemy of our safety, we tend to look at life as a series of potentially harmful events that one endures and constantly recovers from. Unpredictability gives us the opportunity to capitalize on new and unexpected situations, and allow us to reach for a goal that had once been beyond our imagination. When you view the fluctuating nature of our business in this way, while understanding that you have the ability to choose the appropriate strategy for each state of your business productivity, you will remain effective where others fail, calm where others are frantic, visionary where others are simply racked with futility. Understanding the fluctuating nature of your business is to understand the deeper meaning of success as a continuum that reaches equilibrium only when its leader has accepted that our efforts require constant analysis and creative insight.

THE 3 STRENGTHS

The process of making your personal training business productive and profitable will test your tenacity, willfulness, and creativity. You will rely not only on strategy, but also on your ability to manage and interpret data, and will need to be able to pull the trigger on a decision that can switch your tactical focus on a weekly, and sometimes a daily, basis. Proficiency will require experience, but mastery will require time.

However, regardless of your level of proficiency and mastery, there will still be times when all your constructs, plans, insights, and proven methods fall short of what is needed. At such times, when your discipline is not enough, and you have desperation in abundance, you can only rely on your proven strengths. Clarity of thought may not be so easy to come by, and constructing a plan may not be in the cards because there simply is not enough time. At such times, you can only rely on your proven strengths.

Strength is an attribute that can be reliably and predictably utilized in difficult situations. When there is a shortage of clients, when productivity is low, and there seems to be no end in sight, vision and strategy may waver, plans may get thrown out the window, but your strengths will never leave you. There are 3 categories of strength:

- Subject Mastery
- Connectability
- Ambition

For such times, it is important to know your strengths.

The most important reason why you should absolutely know your strengths, especially during difficult periods, is because your thoughts will have a tendency to wander, in search of relief from the pressure of running a business that is verifiably under-performing. Your mind will wander in search of a focus, and when it wanders, it will tend to look at the past. You may remember your failures, more than your successes. There are many trainers who can tell you in perfect detail the cause and effect of their failures. In fact, there are those who exploit this level of storytelling for a profit, by utilizing the tired formula of having grown from the experience without having an effective measurement to quantify it. Avoid this at all costs; half of your energy will be sapped by having to prove how the past will not be repeated, as opposed to devoting your full energy to a future that can be more profitable.

Your success is built on a vision of the future that has yet to happen and is full of possibility. It is not built from lessons of the past—let failure rest where it belongs, in the minds of those who choose to spend their energies cataloguing them. Your mind should be focused on success, and for that to happen, you should have a singular focus on your individual strengths. Failure occurs only when we choose to not use our strengths. A simple way of understanding the role of your strengths in managing the unpredictable nature of business is to answer a simple question: of those 3 strengths, which one will make your business impenetrable and unassailable?

Before you answer that question, it is important to define what each strength means, and why they are important.

SUBJECT MASTERY

This particular strength is characterized by an unassailable knowledge of the subject of your field—technical expertise in exercise science and the human anatomy. This is the trainer who knows every nuance of every principle and theory of the subject. More importantly, this is someone who has taken control of their education to such an extent that their level of precision is, by and large, incomprehensible.

Meeting such individuals, one cannot help but be in utter and complete awe of their accomplishments and their constant need to improve. Such individuals are called *autodidacts*—their true calling in life is to master their subject.

This strength becomes a key component to driving success because it gives you the confidence that you can deliver your product and service *better* than anyone else. This strength makes you fearless when it comes assessing current competition—when in doubt, you know you are the best.

CONNECTABILITY

This strength refers to your *passion to share* your knowledge. Sometimes this passion can translate into a type of compulsive behavior—you cannot help but analyze someone's posture, or give friendly advice about nutrition and recovery. Connectability is a combination of two important components of leadership—competence and likeability. The trainer who shares their knowledge generously gives the client the opportunity to connect with them, and sometimes succeeds in arousing the same level of excitement about fitness. This strength makes you fearless when it comes to approaching your intended market—you know that no matter the result you will have shared their knowledge and excitement, which is a primary ingredient in driving the success of marketing campaigns.

AMBITION

This strength is characterized by the constant need to be better— with a key emphasis on the word *constant*. True ambition, in its purest form, is accompanied by a nagging but effective amount of dissatisfaction in your achievements. Those who utilize this particular strength effectively and at the highest levels are capable of balancing just the right amount of enjoyment of and dissatisfaction with their work so that they enjoy the results enough to reap the benefits, but only long enough so that the flame of their ambitions are not quelled by their current victories. Their hunger for 'more' is constant but manageable.

Ambition makes you fearless in the face of your detractors, bad returns, and ridicule. At times, it can even help you bravely face impending failure; it makes you indifferent to victory and failure because you are going to do what you are going to do, no matter what. There is simply no stopping the ambitious individual. They are impervious to distress, because they believe that the only accountability is self-accountability, and that the only directives worth following are those that are self-directed.

USING YOUR STRENGTHS

Looking at the descriptions of these three strengths, it becomes apparent that you must possess all three as driving factors in your success. It is important, however, to determine which one to use when your business is in a downturn, and you have switched strategies to rebuild and revamp your business. Determine which is your most reliable strength, for the simple reason that time is your limiting factor and resource and it is important to turn your business around as quickly as possible.

The key to picking your strength (ironically) is to review your history, but using the key criteria of determining when you utilized that particular strength *most effectively* during a particularly stressful phase in your life. For example, if you are particularly adept at subject mastery, and you recall a time when you were absolutely the best given a particular scenario, this particular review of your *effectiveness history* should have the criteria not so much of how much you benefitted, but how much you *endured*. Enduring a particular scenario utilizing a key strength means that the strength you possess allowed you the opportunity to develop that key strength. You can then review that scenario again, and identify the key factors outside of your strength that determined its success or failure. Once you recognize the level at which you were able to utilize your strength efficiently, and identify the key factors that colluded to produce success or failure (i.e. economic and market factors, availability of resources, efficiency of supply chain, luck, etc.), you will have essentially created the possibility of utilizing the same strength in the same environment but with *different factors*.

To a certain extent, one can argue that this can be a form of analyzing failure. I would argue that it is not an analysis of failure, but rather a study of strength.

IT AIN'T OVER

"I'm so nervous, what if I forget what I want to say?" Ryan asked me. She had been the number one producer for our club for 12 months in a row, and she was about to receive a special commendation from our regional managers in front of her team. I been had asked to say a few words to her team.

"Well, if you forget, I'm sure you'll find another way to say what you want to say, right? It's from your heart."

She smiled and gave me a hug. "I want to thank you, for everything you have done for me, our team, for everyone. You've done so much, I just want you to know that I think you're the best."

I nodded and hugged her back. "You'll be great, you always were."

When she received her award, the entire team stood up for her in applause. Some were chanting her name, and the room was filled with much rejoicing. There was every reason to be happy, because she had accomplished so much for herself and her team. She had given them an example of how to succeed in this challenging profession, which gave them the motivation to believe that it was possible for all of them. Sometimes the only way to get something done is to first show them that it can be done. Ryan, through her success, showed all of them how it is done.

"My friends, thank you so much. This is an honor, it really is. I can't believe that you're all here, that our regionals are here, and that all of us are together. This award is so great, but it really is for all of us. You all inspire me, and I can't thank this team enough for helping me, for being my inspiration, for just everything!"

"You know, this isn't an easy thing, is it? We all work hard. Every day I see all of you just pushing yourselves. Even the new guys work extra hard, and I know not everyone sees it. I see the new guy always smiling and handing out towels, even though he hasn't gotten a new client in 3 weeks. I see the other veterans coming in everyday, sometimes before the club opens and until the club closes. And you know what? That's not on a report. All a report does is tell you how many sessions you've done or how much money you're going to make. That just breaks my heart, because yes those reports are important, but to me you're more than that. You're more than just a number to me."

"You sure about that?!" Tank called out teasingly. Her teammates laughed, and so did Ryan.

"You know me Tank! I'll get you for that! But do you know what I'm saying? You're not a number, you're a person of value. You all chose this profession because you value yourself to do what you love. And I want all of you to achieve the same kind of success that I have. And the only way you can do that is to not give up...on yourself. Everyone else will, they just will. That's just how people are. But you, YOU can't give up on yourself. You have to make yourself worth it. Maybe other people will see you as a number, but you have to see yourself as a person of intelligence, emotion, and integrity. Maybe they'll say you're just trying to steal their money, but you're not. You care about people, how they walk, how they train, how they feel about themselves, even if you're completely broke. I know a lot of people don't see that, but I see that. I want you to know that I see you, I see you trying to inspire everyone even though they don't appreciate you and they think you're lazy and superficial. I see you for who you really are. And I want you to see who you really are, right? Maybe other people will not value you, but you have to value you. Maybe no one will believe in you, but you have to always believe in you. A lot of people won't really see you as a professional, they'll think you're good for nothing, but professionalism has nothing to do with the money you make, or the kind of job or degree you have. It is about conduct, how you carry yourself in whatever job you happen to hold. You can take pride in the fact that you are not doing this for the money. You are doing this to really help people, because you really care about helping other people. You'll want to quit, I know the feeling. But right now I hope you are understand when I say that you should always believe in yourself, your worth, your level of professionalism, no matter what happens. You're doing good things. You're worth it! Thank you so much!!"

Her teammates rose again to their feet, and ran to Ryan to hug her. There was so much joy in their faces. And in that moment I knew that Ryan understood. It really is worth it. Because she learned that she is worth it.

INTENSITY AND PERSISTENCE PRINCIPLES

It is necessary to constantly ensure that your business is progressing in a way that either meets or exceeds the expectations that you have set for it. However, as the owner and leader of your business, you need a way to insure you are the primary driving force of its success. There are many complex approaches towards self-management that range from the philosophical to the psychological, to the spiritual—all of which are outside of the scope of this book. However, management principles do not only apply to the business you run. They can effectively be applied to how you manage yourself. As much as you manage your integral and potential clients, you can similarly manage three aspects of yourself that can be observed, analyzed, and guided.

- Thoughts
- Words
- Action

If your thoughts, words, and actions are managed so that they align with each other, all three work effectively together towards a common goal. However, if they are not, it is important to understand and ultimately resolve the cause of the disconnect.

The two guiding principles that can help manage these three aspects of yourself are *intensity* and *persistence*. For example:

You are a startup that needs 10 new clients over the next two months. With this goal in mind, you create a series of tasks and procedures to ensure that you reach this particular goal on time or ahead of schedule. You are ready, willing, and able to complete this task.

As simple as this plan may sound, the challenge arises when you realize that there are 24 hours in the day, 5-8 of which are devoted to sleep. 1-2 hours are devoted to training, and another 2 hours (divided throughout the day) are devoted to eating. With a total of 8-12 hours devoted to other necessary aspects of your life, this leaves about 12-14 hours to devote to work, leisure, and routine tasks. During those hours, your level of intensity as it pertains to your tasks can be measured by asking 3 simple questions:

- How much time are you devoting to *thinking* about getting new clients?
- How much time are you devoting to *talking* about getting new clients?
- How much time are you devoting to the processes necessary to *acquiring* new clients?

The answers to these questions will show you whether your thoughts, words, and actions are duly aligned with the objective we have set out for the next two months. The level of intensity that one devotes towards achieving this goal can easily be measured by how often one thinks about, talks about, and actually goes about attaining it. If you are devoting roughly 8 hours of your day towards the achievement of your goal, your level of intensity is obviously higher than if you were devoting only 8 minutes towards the same goal. One can logically infer that if one were to devote such a concentrated effort, with all things being equal, there is a greater chance that you will achieve your goal.

The other factor in success is *persistence*—how long can you think, talk, and act in this manner?

Like a potential client who goes all out in their training in the first two weeks of January, only to fizzle out by February, one can maintain a high level of intensity towards a significant goal for a brief time. The persistence principle measures the *duration* of this intensity, which can also determine the success of the endeavor. If during the two month timeline of attaining 10 clients, your level of intensity wanes at the 20-day mark, chances are your thoughts, words, and actions will start to be less and less directed toward achieving the goal, and more about matters that have nothing to do with it. When you think, talk, and act as if you want something intensely, for a long period of time, there is a high probability that you will get what you want. If you find yourself thinking, talking and acting on your goal sporadically, there is a good chance you will not get where you want to be, for a very simple reason: there's a good chance you are thinking and talking about *something else*.

Intensity and persistence are effective ways of managing yourself relative to a goal that you have set out for yourself. If your focus veers away from your vision and your strategic objectives, your level of effectiveness will be directly affected. You will miss opportunities and fail to capitalize if, for a split-second, your mind goes elsewhere.

THINKING STRATEGICALLY

As your business grows and succeeds, your perspective on many things will change, because the challenges you will face will force you to dig deep into yourself to find the skills and strengths that you need in order to overcome. At times, you may find yourself creating the necessary strengths and skills on the spot, simply because that is what the survival of your business demands.

The key benefit of succeeding in business, from the perspective of personal development, is that you have learned how to think *strategically*. As a successful personal trainer, you will find that you will have developed the crucial ability to anticipate scenarios and potential challenges simply because you will have gone through so many of them before, and you will be able to begin to plan for them. You will develop the uncanny ability to foresee potential scenarios before others do, and start preliminary planning for them, should they occur. When they do occur, you will succeed in taking advantage of the opportunity to the fullest, because you developed and honed a plan for its arrival many months or even years before its time.

In other words, by mastering the challenges and fluctuations of business by strategic thinking and foresight, you will have developed the most important skill in business and in life: *luck*. What looks like luck to others is, in fact, an opportunity that is taken advantage of by a master strategist, someone who has honed their skills for years with little recognition and acknowledgement, until the necessary elements have fallen into place. To the observer, the master strategist will always seem lucky. Repeated success, when closely studied, is the result of an invisible mechanism, silently and invisibly whirring continuously just beneath the surface. That mechanism is the master strategist and how they think. That master strategist is you.

SUCCESS
WITH
THE 4C METHOD

Technical Expertise

- Assessment
- Program Design (Macro)
- Complimentary Session

Business Development and Strategy

- Core Values/Vision/Mission/ Strategic Objectives/Planning/ Tactical Switches/Targets
- 4 Business Models
- 3 Strengths
- Intensity and Persistence Principles

Customer Care

- PACT
- TACT
- Likeability

Sales

- 4 Musts
- 3 Types of Sales
- 3 High-Percentage Objections

Give yourself the time to closely and carefully examine everything that you have learned, so that you can more carefully examine what you are hoping to achieve in this field. Your aim is your direction, your competencies are your sails. Utilizing the 4 Competencies Method will allow you to define your success, clarify the necessary steps, and give you the courage to absorb and overcome the inherent setbacks that occur daily in our business. The purpose of this method and this book is to give you the necessary panorama of your chosen ground so that you may boldly enter it and definitively conquer the field. More ambitiously, this method will give you the important tools for your success, and perhaps encourage you to create and improvise your own, as you are dealt with your own challenges and opportunities.

On a sage note, your success will not be defined by your ability to implement what you have learned here, but rather by how your own instinctive process of unraveling your own unique challenges will be revitalized, sharpened, and emboldened by this approach. Problems, more often than not, tend to be predictable, but how they are unraveled relies on the individual insight and brilliance of the person in the midst of its confusion and its Gordian enigma.

This method outlines the essential problem of the trainer when entering the field—how to succeed with a high level of technical expertise that is combined with intelligent customer care, so that the client is willingly inspired to overcome their own challenges, while managing a successful personal training business.

What this method cannot give you, and what any method of success cannot give you, is the value that may or may not be inherent in the achievement of your overall mission. A method can be crystal clear in its description of a problem, and perhaps be even clearer in its proven approach to understanding and dissolving it. It cannot, however, give you the sense of accomplishment that you could potentially experience when everything is completed.

In other words, the 4C Method can get you to success, but it cannot give *meaning to your* success. To give your success meaning, it will take more than learning a proven method. It will, in fact, require a more thorough examination of your profession and yourself. More specifically what your profession purports to accomplish with your eventual success.

A common lament in our industry is that should our clients only listen to the advice that we give them, adhere to the program that we have designed, and comply with the lifestyle advice that we have recommended, they would succeed in achieving the results that they are looking for—the results that they are paying us to help them achieve. However, as we have discussed in previous chapters, it is more strongly advisable that we view ourselves as partners in their journey of progress and achievement, as opposed to purveyors of unassailable expertise, because their search for change is actually a search for inspiration that leads to definitive and transformative action. An expert can be right and impressively so, but only an inspirational figure who partners in their journey will motivate them. The training program that, to a certain extent, encapsulates the knowledge that we have amassed, in this light, must not be approached as a checklist of tasks, but more as a set of parameters within which the client can freely explore and individualize, so that it motivates them to action. We are not looking for compliance; we are looking to show them what we think is possible.

When viewed from this perspective, we avoid the result of the previously mentioned lament: we judge our clients based on their compliance. It is important to avoid this way of thinking, not only because it will affect the partnership, but because this line of thinking determines who we are, how we affect those around us, and how we view the world we live in. A trainer who judges their client based on their compliance to a program is not capable of partnering. That trainer may be good at writing programs, good at telling people what to do, but their influence is limited because no one is actually listening to them.

People listen to inspiration, not instruction. People listen to leaders, not experts. The expert may have the best instructions, but they are doomed to irrelevance if they cannot turn their knowledge into a powerful message. As leaders with the ability to connect and partner, our level of influence is measured by how we help our clients change their lives.

A fully developed adult is one who has outgrown the seeming usefulness of Reactivity—of judgment and separation—and has developed, instead, the skill of fully comprehending a situation, and being decisive in one's action. And it is this type of decisiveness that determines the quality of one's life, because it is authentic decisiveness that achieves life-changing results. We do not transform the lives of our clients by judging them; we help them take control of their lives by helping them develop the skill of being decisive, thereby transforming their own lives.

You change a person's life not by changing how they act, but by changing how they *think*. You change the way a person thinks not by expertise that you generously dole out—you cannot change a person's mind by *telling* them to change their mind. You can only change a person's mind by being the successful embodiment of the core values you represent and the choices you have made—you are the representation of *how you think*. You are the representation of what you believe in. When you share your knowledge, that knowledge is best processed when the source of that knowledge is its direct representation. More importantly, that knowledge has to have made you humbler, more compassionate, and more connected. In other words, you become someone worth listening to, someone worth believing in. Someone who believes in quality, excellence, and resilience, the bearer of knowledge, capable of applying it judiciously in their every word, thought, and action. How you think, and how that creates the physical reality of your life, impacts the clients you train because they cannot help but *believe in you*. Their belief in you is based on your level of success as measured by the life you are living— and that is one of main the things they want. They want to be inspired by someone who is capable of turning belief into action, action into achievement, and achievement into a fulfilling experience of the life they are living.

Your success is fundamentally based on an uncompromising belief in yourself. Your clients receive the residual effect of that success—and that is ultimately what they are looking for. It is, in fact, what everyone is looking for.

Every person who joins a gym has a set of goals in mind. As previously discussed, these goals, when properly outlined and determined during the assessment, tells a story of what the client envisions when they start the process of training with you. Every journey starts with a step in the direction of its intended destination, but the destination in and of itself does not embody the nature of that journey. The challenges and benchmarks that demarcate the program create the impression that the client is on a mountain trek to the top of a very high and escalating peak. We are their knowing guide, to a mountain that we ourselves have travelled to and conquered. However, when we examine our own journey, we did not set out to conquer a mountain. Perhaps, on the surface, it seemed like conquest, but inside us, in the truth of us, we were not climbing—we were simply searching. As we partner with our clients, what will resonate deeply within us is that they are searching for the same thing that everyone is searching for.

Everyone is searching for something to believe in. What you have found, through your own abilities, your own determination, and your own experiences, is that you achieved everything in your life because you believed, most of all, in *yourself.* Your search began with belief, and what you found was self-belief. Every client that you partner with, teach, guide, and lead is on the same search, on the same path, headed towards that most significant and most elusive of all goals—to find a way to believe in oneself once again. For in that belief, one finds possibility in what was once impossible. For everything that cannot be done, one simply gets it done.

For every client that achieves their goal, they believe in themselves a little more. Rep for rep, mile for mile, they are transforming their lives because they are learning to believe in their ability to control their destiny. That is the power of self-belief. It teaches us to believe in ourselves again, in what is possible, in what has always been within our reach, to embolden ourselves to harness our rightful ability to live the lives we are meant to live. That is our calling, that is our cause, and that is our message. What we do is more than fitness. It is far beyond it, and now we must recognize it. To be a part of helping someone believe in themselves that they become capable of living their lives with courage and dignity, is what makes what we do respectable, noble, and, in the final reckoning, worthwhile.

ABOUT THE AUTHOR

R olando Garcia III has been described as one of the top managers in the fitness industry. Using the system he created, he has prepared and developed fitness teams as well as individual professionals for the demands and rigors of the fitness profession, which led to their subsequent success. He currently manages an elite team of coaches for a luxury fitness facility, which is located in Manhattan, NY. He has been featured on Forbes, *The NY POST, Self Magazine,* and *Athlete's Quarterly.*